The Healthy Power Pressure Cooker XL Cookbook

105 Nourishing Electric Pressure Cooker Recipes
For Clean eating, Gluten free, Paleo, Low carb,
Dairy free, Vegetarian And Vegan Diets

NAOMI BECKER

ISBN-13: 978-1540757708
ISBN-10: 1540757706

DEDICATION

To all home cooking and healthy living enthusiasts.

.

TABLE OF CONTENT

INTRODUCTION

These days, pressure cookers require little introduction. Many popular brands are on the market and they provide different levels of performance and user satisfaction. The Power Pressure Cooker XL has stood the test of time and is one of the best you can find on the on the market. The popularity of the Power Pressure Cooker (XL and Pro versions) is increasing rapidly because of the advance functions provided. It is a multipurpose kitchen appliance that can be used for a variety of cooking tasks such as pressure cooking, slow cooking, canning, steaming, browning and more.

This cookbook provides you with 105 healthy electric pressure cooker recipes and step by step instructions on how to cook them in your Power

Pressure Cooker XL or Pro. These delicious recipes can be enjoyed by all. No matter your taste preference or dietary need, there are several recipes that will satisfy you in this collection. These dietary needs include Clean eating, Gluten free, Paleo, Low carb, Dairy free, Vegetarian and Vegan.

The Power Pressure Cooker XL is the ideal appliance for cooking healthy meals quickly and very easily. It cooks food up to 70% faster than traditional cooking methods. Minimal water is required for cooking and the Power Pressure Cooker XL traps steam within the food with the flavor infusion technology. These locks in the moisture into your food resulting in better flavor and nutritious value.

The ease of use of the Power Pressure Cooker XL is a benefit that is appreciated by many users. You can cook a variety of meals at the push of a button. These one-touch settings cover groups of food like meat, beans, rice, fish, vegetables, soup or stews. Just combine the ingredients, push the applicable button and the Power Pressure Cooker XL does the rest. You can also adjust the time of each preset program according to specific cooking requirements.

The technology of the Power Pressure Cooker XL will ensure that you have delicious and healthy food each time you cook. Precious nutrients and vitamins are locked into the food, meat and seafood get intense flavor and vegetables are tender-crisp. With the 105 recipes in this book, you will always know what to cook any day of the week.

Power Pressure Cooker XL Built In Safety

Lid Safety Device – This prevents the buildup of pressure if the lid is not properly closed and also prevents the opening of the lid until all the pressure in the unit is released.

Pressure And Temperature Sensor Controls – This regulates heat and pressure by either deactivating or activating the power supply.

Back-up Safety Release Valve – In the unlikely event of the malfunction of the Temperature/Pressure Sensor device, leading to excessive pressure buildup, this "Back-Up" kicks in automatically and the pressure is released.

Clog Resistant Feature – This simply prevents the blocking of the steam release port by food.

Spring-Loaded Safety Pressure Release – A further back up safety feature that kicks in if those listed above fail. It is a device under the heating element that lowers the Inner Pot and detaches it from the Rubber Gasket. This leads to the automatic escape of steam and pressure.

Temperature Cut-Off Device – This cuts off power supply if the unit malfunctions and the internal temperature rises abnormally.

Tips For Using The Power Pressure Cooker XL

You Can Cook With Any Of The Preset Buttons

All the Power Cook XL preset buttons (apart from Canning) cook at the same pressure so you can use anyone of them to cook your food. Just choose the preset button with the closest cooking time to your recipe and add the necessary time.

Adjusting The Cooking Time

The Time Adjust button enables you to manually adjust the cook time no matter the preset button that you choose.

Sautéing Or Browning Food

Browning is done with the lid off. A sauté button is not provided in the Power Pressure Cooker XL but it is present in the Power Cooker Pro. To brown or sauté, simply leave the unit uncovered and press any of the preset

3

buttons. For the recipes in this book, the CHICKEN/MEAT button is used for sautéing/browning.

Note: Many of the recipes in this books ask you to sauté or brown certain ingredients before combining with the rest of the ingredients. Sometimes, you may choose not to do this to save time and just combine everything at once. However, the outcome will not be as delicious and flavorful.

Slow Cooking

You can cook a variety of slow cooker recipes with the Slow Cook feature.

Cooking Frozen Food

Frozen food can be cooked in the Power Pressure Cooker XL. You just need to add 10 minutes to the cooking time.

Converting Other Electric Pressure Cooker Recipes

You don't have to increase the cooking time when using other electric pressure cooker recipes. Even with the seemingly low PSI, the Power Pressure Cooker XL gets food done within the same time with other electric pressure cookers.

However, you will have to add about 20 percent additional cooking time if you are using recipes designed for stove top pressure cookers.

Releasing The Pressure

At the end of the cooking time, simply switch the pressure release valve to open. This will quickly release the pressure. If you want natural release, do not turn the pressure release valve. The cooker switches to Keep warm automatically and pressure will start decreasing on its own.

BREAKFAST AND BRUNCH

Easy Breakfast Polenta (Clean eating, Gluten free, Dairy free, Vegan)

Preparation time: 5 minutes

Cooking time: 10 minutes

Servings: 6

Ingredients:

1 1/2 cups polenta flour

1 teaspoon salt

5 cups vegetable broth

Directions:

1. Insert the inner pot into your Power Cooker then add the broth with salt. Press the CHICKEN/MEAT button and bring to a boil.

2. Add the polenta flour gradually, while stirring in one direction with a wooden spoon until everything has been added.

3. Cover the Power Cooker, lock the lid then turn the pressure release valve to closed.

4. Next, press the WARM/CANCEL button then choose the RICE/RISOTTO button and adjust the time to 9 minutes.

5. When the time is up, the Power Cooker will switch to KEEP WARM automatically. Turn the pressure release valve to open.

6. Wait until the steam is released completely before opening the cover.

7. Whisk the polenta until smooth. Transfer to a serving pan or serve in individual dishes.

Breakfast Hash (Clean eating, Gluten free, Dairy free)

Preparation time: 20 minutes

Cooking time: 15 minutes

Servings: 4

Ingredients:

2 pounds potatoes, peeled, shredded

8 ounces crumbled sausage

2 tablespoons olive oil

2 tablespoons finely chopped basil

1/4 cup chicken broth

Salt, to taste

Pepper, to taste

Directions:

1. Insert the inner pot into your Power Cooker, press the CHICKEN/MEAT button and add the olive oil. Add the potatoes, salt and pepper. Cook and stir occasionally for 5 minutes.

2. Add the basil, sausage and chicken broth. Stir to combine.

3. Cover the Power Cooker, lock the lid then turn the pressure release valve to closed.

4. Next, press the WARM/CANCEL button then choose the BEANS/LENTILS button and adjust the time to 7 minutes.

5. When the time is up, the Power Cooker will switch to KEEP WARM automatically. Turn the pressure release valve to open.

6. Wait until the steam is released completely before opening the cover.

7. Serve hot with scrambled eggs and toast.

Crunchy Steel Cut Oats (Clean eating, Dairy free, Vegan)

The Power Cooker cooks crunchy steel cut oats very easily.

Preparation time: 2 minutes

Cooking time: 5 minutes

Servings: 3

Ingredients:

1/2 cup steel cut oats

1 tablespoon vegetable oil

2 cups water

Salt, to taste

Directions:

1. Insert the inner pot into your Power Cooker then add all the ingredients.

2. Cover the Power Cooker, lock the lid then turn the pressure release valve to closed.

3. Next, press the RICE/RISOTTO button (6 minutes).

4. When the time is up, the Power Cooker will switch to KEEP WARM automatically. Turn the pressure release valve to open.

5. Wait until the steam is released completely before opening the cover.

6. Stir, then let sit for 1-2 minutes.

7. Serve with desired toppings and sweeteners.

Breakfast Brown Rice Risotto (Clean eating, Gluten free, Dairy free, Vegan)

Preparation time: 5 minutes

Cooking time: 25 minutes

Servings: 4

Ingredients:

2 tablespoons margarine

1 1/2 cups short grain brown rice

2 medium bananas, lightly mashed

1/3 cup brown sugar

1/4 teaspoon salt

1 1/2 teaspoons cinnamon

3 cups light coconut milk

1 cup dry white wine

Chopped walnuts, for garnish

Directions:

1. Insert the inner pot into your Power Cooker, press the CHICKEN/MEAT button and add the margarine.

2. When the margarine is melted, add the rice and cook with constant stirring for about 3 minutes.

3. Stir in the bananas, sugar, salt, cinnamon, coconut milk and wine.

4. Cover the Power Cooker, lock the lid then turn the pressure release valve to closed.

5. Next, press the WARM/CANCEL button then choose the RICE/RISOTTO button and adjust the time to 20 minutes.

6. When the time is up, the Power Cooker will switch to KEEP WARM automatically. Turn the pressure release valve to open.

7. Wait until the steam is released completely before opening the cover.

8. Serve, garnished with chopped walnuts.

Breakfast Burrito (Clean eating, Low carb)

Fills you up for days when there is a lot of work to do.

Preparation time: 15 minutes

Cooking time: 10 minutes

Servings: 4

Ingredients:

2 tablespoons of olive oil

4 eggs

1/2 cup chopped red onion

1 green chili pepper, seeded, diced

12 cherry tomatoes, diced

Salt to taste

1/4 cup water

4 flour tortillas

2 avocados, peeled, pitted, and mashed

1 cup shredded Cheddar cheese

1/4 cup ketchup

Directions:

1. Insert the inner pot into your Power Cooker, press the CHICKEN/MEAT button and add the olive oil.

2. Beat the eggs together in a bowl and pour into the Power Cooker. Cook and stir for 2 minutes.

3. Add onion, chili pepper, tomatoes and salt to taste. Pour in 1/4 cup of water.

4. Cover the Power Cooker, lock the lid then turn the pressure release valve to closed.

5. Next, press the WARM/CANCEL button then choose the FISH/VEGETABLE button and adjust the time to 7 minutes.

6. When the time is up, the Power Cooker will switch to KEEP WARM automatically. Turn the pressure release valve to open.

7. Wait until the steam is released completely before opening the cover.

8. Meanwhile Microwave flour tortillas for 30 seconds.

9. Lay tortillas, one at a time on a flat surface. Layer 1/4 of the egg mixture, 1/4 of the avocados and 1/4 of the Cheddar cheese on the middle of the tortilla. Repeat with the remaining tortilla then roll them up.

10. Serve with ketchup.

Berries And Almond Steel Cut Oats (Clean eating, Dairy free, Vegan)

Preparation time: 5 minutes

Cooking time: 5 minutes

Servings: 4

Ingredients:

1 cup steel cut oats

1 1/2 cups almond milk

1/2 cup water

3 tablespoons maple syrup

1 cup mixed berries

1/4 cup sliced almonds

1 teaspoon vanilla extract

Directions:

1. Insert the inner pot into your Power Cooker then add all the ingredients and mix together.

2. Cover the Power Cooker, lock the lid then turn the pressure release valve to closed.

3. Next, press the RICE/RISOTTO button (6 minutes).

4. When the time is up, the Power Cooker will switch to KEEP WARM automatically. Turn the pressure release valve to open.

5. Wait until the steam is released completely before opening the cover.

Quick And Easy Breakfast Quinoa (Clean eating, Gluten free, Dairy free, Vegan)

Get some protein and healthy fiber into your body with this light and fluffy breakfast cereal.

Preparation time: 5 minutes

Cooking time: 2 minutes

Servings: 4-6

Ingredients:

1 1/2 cups quinoa, well rinsed, drained

2 1/4 cups water or broth

1 tablespoon vegetable oil

2 tablespoons maple syrup

2 teaspoons turmeric

2 teaspoons cumin

1/4 teaspoon ground cinnamon

1/2 teaspoon vanilla

1 teaspoon salt (optional)

Optional garnish: sliced almonds, chopped pecans or fresh berries

Directions:

1. Insert the inner pot into your Power Cooker then add all the ingredients and mix together.

2. Cover the Power Cooker, lock the lid then turn the pressure release valve to closed.

3. Next, press the FISH/VEGETABLE button (2 minutes).

4. When the time is up, the Power Cooker will switch to KEEP WARM automatically. Turn the pressure release valve to open.

5. Wait until the steam is released completely before opening the cover.

6. Fluff the quinoa with a fork. Serve drizzled with maple and garnished with desired toppings.

Breakfast Potato And Mixed Herbs (Clean eating, Gluten free, Dairy free, Vegan)

Preparation time: 10 minutes

Cooking time: 15 minutes

Servings: 4

Ingredients:

2 tablespoons olive oil

1 medium onion, diced

8 medium potatoes, quartered

1/2 cup water

1/4 teaspoon dried basil

1/4 teaspoon dried oregano

1/4 teaspoon dried thyme

1/4 teaspoon dried rosemary

1/4 teaspoon dried sage

Salt, to taste

Pepper, to taste

1/2 lemon

Directions:

1. Insert the inner pot into your Power Cooker, press the CHICKEN/MEAT button and add the olive oil. Sauté onions for about 5 minutes.

2. Add potatoes and brown evenly on all sides.

3. Add the water, herbs, salt and pepper. Stir to coat.

4. Cover the Power Cooker, lock the lid then turn the pressure release valve to closed.

5. Next, press the WARM/CANCEL button then choose the BEANS/LENTILS button (5 minutes).

6. When the time is up, the Power Cooker will switch to KEEP WARM automatically. Turn the pressure release valve to open.

7. Wait until the steam is released completely before opening the cover.

8. Serve, drizzled with lemon juice.

Oatmeal With Carrot (Clean eating, Dairy free, Vegan)

Preparation time: 10 minutes

Cooking time: 13 minutes

Servings: 6

Ingredients:

1 tablespoon vegan butter

1 cup steel cut oats

1 cup grated carrots

4 cups water

3 tablespoons maple syrup

1 teaspoon pumpkin pie spice

1/4 teaspoon salt

2 teaspoons cinnamon

1/4 cup chopped dried apricots

1/2 cup slivered almonds

1/2 cup raisins

Directions:

1. Insert the inner pot into your Power Cooker, press the CHICKEN/MEAT button and add the butter.

2. When butter melts, add the oats and cook, constantly stirring for about 3 minutes.

3. Add the carrots, water, maple syrup, pumpkin pie spice and salt.

16

4. Cover the Power Cooker, lock the lid then turn the pressure release valve to closed.

5. Next, press the WARM/CANCEL button then choose the RICE/RISOTTO button and adjust the time to 10 minutes.

6. When the time is up, the Power Cooker will switch to KEEP WARM automatically. Turn the pressure release valve to open.

7. Wait until the steam is released completely before opening the cover.

8. Stir in the cinnamon, apricots, almonds and raisins. Let sit for a few minutes before serving.

SOUPS, STEWS, AND CHILIES

Chicken Enchilada Soup (Clean eating, Gluten free, Paleo, Low carb, Dairy free)

Preparation time: 20 minutes

Cooking time: 10 minutes

Servings: 6

Ingredients:

2 pounds boneless skinless chicken breasts

1 tablespoon extra virgin olive oil

2 cups sliced celery

2 cups sliced carrots

2 garlic cloves, minced

1/2 cup diced yellow onions

1 1/2 teaspoon sea salt

1/2 teaspoon black pepper

2 tablespoons taco seasoning

2 cups cubed butternut squash

1 (18-ounce) jar diced tomatoes

5 cups chicken stock

2 teaspoons lime juice

Cilantro and lime wedges, for serving

Directions:

1. Insert the inner pot into your Power Cooker, press the CHICKEN/MEAT button and add the olive oil. Add celery, carrots, garlic, onions, salt, pepper and taco seasoning. Cook and stir for about 5 minutes.

2. Add the remaining ingredients then stir.

3. Cover the Power Cooker, lock the lid then turn the pressure release valve to closed.

4. Next, press the WARM/CANCEL button then choose the BEANS/LENTILS button (5 minutes).

5. When the time is up, the Power Cooker will switch to KEEP WARM automatically. Turn the pressure release valve to open.

6. Wait until the steam is released completely before opening the cover.

7. Remove the chicken, shred with two forks and return to the Power Cooker.

8. Stir the soup then serve with lime wedges and cilantro.

Easy Minestrone Soup (Clean eating, Dairy free, Vegan)

Preparation time: 10 minutes

Cooking time: 10 minutes

Servings: 4-6

Ingredients:

2 tablespoons olive oil or lard

1 large onion, diced

2 celery stalks, diced

3 garlic cloves, minced

1 large carrot, diced

1 teaspoon of dried oregano

1 teaspoon of dried basil

Sea salt, to taste

Pepper, to taste

4 cups vegetable broth

1 (28-ounce) can whole tomatoes, crushed

1/2 cup fresh spinach, torn into shreds

1 bay leaf

1 cup whole-wheat elbow pasta

1 (15-ounces) can white or cannellini beans

Directions:

1. Insert the inner pot into your Power Cooker, press the CHICKEN/MEAT button and add the olive oil.

2. Add the onion, celery, garlic and carrot. Cook and stir often until vegetables are softened. Add oregano, basil, salt and pepper.

3. Add the vegetable broth, crushed tomatoes, spinach, bay leaf and pasta.

4. Cover the Power Cooker, lock the lid then turn the pressure release valve to closed.

5. Next, press the WARM/CANCEL button then choose the RICE/RISOTTO button (6 minutes).

6. When the time is up, the Power Cooker will switch to KEEP WARM automatically. Turn the pressure release valve to open.

7. Wait until the steam is released completely before opening the cover.

8. Stir in the white beans.

9. Serve, topped with your favorite pesto.

Smoked Sausage And Chicken Stew (Clean eating, Gluten free, Paleo, Low carb, Dairy free)

Preparation time: 10 minutes

Cooking time: 25 minutes

Servings: 6

Ingredients:

1 pound andouille pork sausage

1 pound boneless, skinless chicken breasts

1 tablespoon coconut oil

2 stalks celery

1 medium white onion

2 large carrots

3 green bell peppers

6 garlic cloves

6 cups chopped tomatoes

2 cups bone broth

1 teaspoon thyme

1/2 teaspoon crushed red pepper flakes

1/2 teaspoon smoked paprika

1/4 teaspoon cayenne

1 teaspoon salt

1/4 teaspoon black pepper

1 bay leaf

1/4 cup parsley

Directions:

1. Insert the inner pot into your Power Cooker, press the CHICKEN/MEAT button and add the coconut oil.

2. When the coconut oil has melted, add the sausage and chicken and cook through. Remove sausage and chicken from the pot and set aside.

3. Add the celery, onion, carrots and bell peppers. Sauté the vegetables with occasional stirring for about 5 minutes.

4. Add the garlic, chopped tomatoes and broth then let simmer.

5. Meanwhile, slice the sausage and chicken into bite size pieces. Add them to the pot then add the spices and parsley. Stir to combine.

6. Cover the Power Cooker, lock the lid then turn the pressure release valve to closed.

7. Next, press the WARM/CANCEL button then choose the SOUP/STEW button (10 minutes).

8. When the time is up, the Power Cooker will switch to KEEP WARM automatically. Turn the pressure release valve to open.

9. Wait until the steam is released completely before opening the cover.

10. Serve warm

Chicken And White Bean Chili (Clean eating, Gluten free, Low carb)

An infusion of great flavors in just 35 minutes.

Preparation time: 15 minutes

Cooking time: 20 minutes

Servings: 6-8

Ingredients:

2 pounds boneless, skinless chicken breasts, cubed

1 1/2 cup dried white kidney beans, soaked overnight, rinsed

2 tablespoon olive

1 garlic cloves, minced

1 medium onion, chopped

4.5 ounces mild green chilies, drained, chopped

1/2 teaspoon cayenne pepper

2 teaspoon ground cumin

2 teaspoon ground oregano

6 cups chicken stock

Topping:

1/2 cup fresh cilantro - torn

1 cup cheddar cheese, shredded

Directions:

1. Insert the inner pot into your Power Cooker, press the CHICKEN/MEAT button and add the olive oil.

2. Add onions garlic; cook for about 2 minutes. Add the chicken; cook with occasional stirring until browned.

3. Add the beans, chilies, cayenne pepper, cumin and oregano; cook for 2 minutes. Stir in the chicken stock.

4. Cover the Power Cooker, lock the lid then turn the pressure release valve to closed.

5. Next, press the WARM/CANCEL button then choose the BEANS/LENTILS button and adjust the time to 16 minutes.

6. When the time is up, the Power Cooker will switch to KEEP WARM automatically. Turn the pressure release valve to open.

7. Wait until the steam is released completely before opening the cover.

8. Using a fork or potato masher, mash some of the beans to thicken the soup.

9. Serve, sprinkled with cheddar cheese and topped with cilantro.

Creamy Cauliflower And Fennel Soup (Clean eating, Gluten free, Paleo, Low carb, Dairy free, Vegan)

Creamy, lusciously and comforting.

Preparation time: 10 minutes

Cooking time: 20 minutes

Servings: 4

Ingredients:

1 tablespoon coconut oil

1 white onion, sliced

3 garlic cloves, minced

1 pound cauliflower florets

1 extra large fennel bulb, fronds and stalks removed, chopped

3 cups broth vegetable broth

1 cup coconut milk

2 teaspoons salt

Directions:

1. Insert the inner pot into your Power Cooker, press the CHICKEN/MEAT button and add the coconut oil.

2. Add onions and sauté for 5 minutes. Add garlic, cauliflower and fennel. Cook and stir until vegetables begin to turn golden at the edges, about 5-10 minutes.

3. Pour in the coconut milk, vegetable broth and salt. Stir to combine.

4. Cover the Power Cooker, lock the lid then turn the pressure release valve to closed.

5. Next, press the WARM/CANCEL button then choose the BEANS/LENTILS button (5 minutes).

6. When the time is up, the Power Cooker will switch to KEEP WARM automatically. Turn the pressure release valve to open.

7. Wait until the steam is released completely before opening the cover.

8. Using an immersion blender, puree the soup until smooth and creamy. You can also transfer to a regular blender.

9. Serve hot.

Easy Onion Soup (Clean eating, Gluten free, Paleo, Low carb, Dairy free, Vegan)

Preparation time: 20 minutes

Cooking time: 25 minutes

Servings: 4

Ingredients:

2 tablespoons coconut oil or avocado oil

8 cups yellow onions, chopped

1 tablespoon balsamic vinegar

6 cups vegetable broth

1 teaspoon real salt

2 sprigs fresh thyme

2 bay leaves

Directions:

1. Insert the inner pot into your Power Cooker, press the CHICKEN/MEAT button and add the oil.

2. Add onions and cook with occasional stirring until translucent, about 15 minutes.

3. Stir in the balsamic vinegar, scraping any food on the bottom of the pot. Add the rest of the ingredients .

4. Cover the Power Cooker, lock the lid then turn the pressure release valve to closed.

5. Next, press the WARM/CANCEL button then choose the SOUP/STEW button (10 minutes).

6. When the time is up, the Power Cooker will switch to KEEP WARM automatically. Turn the pressure release valve to open.

7. Wait until the steam is released completely before opening the cover.

8. Remove and discard thyme stems and bay leaves. Blend the soup using a regular or immersion blender.

Chicken Green Chili (Clean eating, Gluten free, Low carb, Dairy free)

Bright, fresh and full of flavor.

Preparation time: 10 minutes

Cooking time: 20 minutes

Servings: 4 - 6

Ingredients:

3 pounds chicken legs, divided into thighs and drumsticks

4 tomatillos, quartered, husks discarded

2 jalapeño or Serrano chilies, chopped roughly, stems discarded

5 poblano peppers, chopped roughly, seeds and stems discarded

6 garlic cloves, peeled

1 medium white onion, chopped roughly

1 tablespoon ground cumin

Kosher salt

1 tablespoon fish sauce

1/2 cup loosely packed fresh cilantro leaves, plus more for garnish

Lime wedges, for serving

Fresh corn tortillas, for serving

Directions:

1. Insert the inner pot into your Power Cooker. Add the chicken, tomatillos, jalapeño peppers, poblano peppers, garlic, cumin and a generous pinch of salt.

2. Press the CHICKEN/MEAT button and heat until gently sizzling.

3. Cover the Power Cooker, lock the lid then turn the pressure release valve to closed.

4. Next, press the WARM/CANCEL button then choose the CHICKEN/MEAT button and adjust the time to 15 minutes.

5. When the time is up, the Power Cooker will switch to KEEP WARM automatically. Turn the pressure release valve to open.

6. Wait until the steam is released completely before opening the cover.

7. Use tongs to remove the chicken and place in a bowl.

8. Add the fish sauce and cilantro to the pot. Use an immersion or standing blender to blend. Taste and add more salt if needed.

9. Return chicken to the sauce (if you like, remove and discard the bones and skin).

10. Serve with tortillas and garnish with lime wedges and cilantro.

Buffalo Chicken Soup (Gluten free, Low carb)

Easy and delicious with just the right amount of flavor.

Preparation time: minutes

Cooking time: 10 minutes

Servings: 2

Ingredients:

2 boneless skinless chicken breasts

1/4 cup diced onion

1 garlic clove, chopped

1/2 cup diced celery

2 tablespoons butter or ghee

3 cups chicken bone broth

1/3 cup hot sauce

1 tablespoon ranch dressing mix

1 cup heavy cream

2 cups cheddar cheese, shredded

Directions:

1. Insert the inner pot into your Power Cooker.

2. Add all the ingredients except the heavy cream and cheese.

3. Cover the Power Cooker, lock the lid then turn the pressure release valve to closed.

4. Next, press the SOUP/STEW button (10 minutes).

5. When the time is up, the Power Cooker will switch to KEEP WARM automatically. Turn the pressure release valve to open.

6. Wait until the steam is released completely before opening the cover.

7. Remove the chicken carefully, shred then return to the pot. Stir in the heavy cream and cheese.

Butternut Squash And Ginger Soup (Clean eating, Gluten free, Paleo, Dairy free, Vegan)

Just combine, boil then puree for a creamy delight.

Preparation time: 5 minutes

Cooking time: 23 minutes

Servings: 6-8

Ingredients:

4 pounds butternut squash, peeled, seeded, cubed

1 tablespoon olive oil

1 large onion, chopped roughly

1 leek, chopped

1/2 cinnamon stick

1/2-inch piece of ginger, peeled, sliced roughly

4 cups vegetable stock

Salt, to taste

Pepper, to taste

Cilantro, chopped

1/2 cup toasted sesame seeds

Directions:

1. Insert the inner pot into your Power Cooker, press the CHICKEN/MEAT button and add the olive oil. Add onions and leek. Cook until onions are soft then add salt and pepper.

2. Push onions aside and add enough butternut squash cubes to cover the bottom of the Power Cooker. Cook with frequent stirring for about 10 minutes.

3. Add the remaining butternut squash, cinnamon, ginger and stock.

4. Cover the Power Cooker, lock the lid then turn the pressure release valve to closed.

5. Next, press the WARM/CANCEL button then choose the SOUP/STEW button and adjust the time to 18 minutes.

6. When the time is up, the Power Cooker will switch to KEEP WARM automatically. Turn the pressure release valve to open.

7. Wait until the steam is released completely before opening the cover.

8. Remove and discard the cinnamon stick.

9. Use an immersion blender or regular blender to puree everything.

10. Serve, garnished with toasted sesame seeds and cilantro.

Simple Tomato Soup (Clean eating, Gluten free, Pal.., Low carb, Dairy free, Vegan)

Easy to prepare and perfect for cold days.

Preparation time: 15 minutes

Cooking time: 25 minutes

Servings: 4-6

Ingredients:

5 cups coarsely chopped fresh tomatoes, with seed and juice

2 tablespoons olive oil

1 medium onion, diced

2 celery ribs, diced

1 large carrot, chopped

1/2 cup vegetable broth

1 teaspoon dried basil

1 teaspoon dried thyme

1 teaspoon salt

1/2 teaspoon freshly ground pepper

3/4 cup coconut cream

Directions:

1. Insert the inner pot into your Power Cooker, press the CHICKEN/MEAT button and add the olive oil. Add onions; cook and stir for 2 minutes. Add celery and carrots; cook and stir for 4 minutes.

2. Add the tomatoes, broth, basil, thyme, salt and pepper.

3. Cover the Power Cooker, lock the lid then turn the pressure release valve to closed.

4. Next, press the WARM/CANCEL button then choose the SOUP/STEW button and adjust the time to 15 minutes.

5. When the time is up, the Power Cooker will switch to KEEP WARM automatically. Turn the pressure release valve to open.

6. Wait until the steam is released completely before opening the cover.

7. Use a regular or immersion blender to puree the soup.

5. Return to the Power Cooker then stir in the coconut cream. Press the CHICKEN/MEAT button and let simmer, uncovered, stirring occasionally for about 3 minutes.

Quick And Easy Lentil Soup (Clean eating, Gluten free, Dairy free, Vegan)
An old favorite cooked quicker in your Power Cooker.

Preparation time: 5 minutes

Cooking time: 15 minutes

Servings: 6

Ingredients:

2 cups brown and/or red lentils, sorted, rinsed

1 tablespoon olive oil

1 cup chopped onions

2 garlic cloves, minced

1 teaspoon ground coriander

1 teaspoons chipotle powder

2 large carrots, sliced

1 pound Yukon Gold or Red potatoes, cubed

2 bay leaves

4 cups water

4 cups vegetable broth

Salt and pepper, to taste

1 bunch spinach, chopped

Directions:

1. Insert the inner pot into your Power Cooker, press the CHICKEN/MEAT button and add the olive oil. Add the onions and garlic; cook and stir for 2 minutes.

2. Add coriander, chipotle powder, carrots and potatoes. Cook and stir for 3 more minutes.

3. Add the bay leaves, water, broth, lentils and a little salt.

4. Cover the Power Cooker, lock the lid then turn the pressure release valve to closed.

5. Next, press the WARM/CANCEL button then choose the BEANS/LENTILS button and adjust the time to 8 minutes..

6. When the time is up, the Power Cooker will switch to KEEP WARM automatically. Turn the pressure release valve to open.

7. Wait until the steam is released completely before opening the cover.

8. Remove and discard the bay leaves.

6. Stir in the spinach, season with salt and pepper to taste. Serve.

Potato, Pea, Leek Soup (Clean eating, Gluten free, Dairy free, Vegan)

Preparation time: 15 minutes

Cooking time: 22 minutes

Servings: 4

Ingredients:

2 tablespoons olive oil

1 pound leeks, washed, chopped finely

1 cup peas

1 pound potatoes, cubed

2 tablespoons fresh parsley, minced

1 pinch dried mint leaves, crumbled

1 cup coconut milk

4 cups vegetable stock or water

Salt, to taste

Pepper, to taste

Directions:

1. Insert the inner pot into your Power Cooker, press the CHICKEN/MEAT button and add the olive oil. Sauté leeks in hot oil until tender, about 8-10 minutes.

2. Add the peas, potatoes, parsley and mint.

3. Stir in the coconut milk and vegetable stock. Add salt and pepper to taste.

4. Cover the Power Cooker, lock the lid then turn the pressure release valve to closed.

5. Next, press the WARM/CANCEL button then choose the BEANS/LENTILS button and adjust the time to 12 minutes.

6. When the time is up, the Power Cooker will switch to KEEP WARM automatically. Turn the pressure release valve to open.

7. Wait until the steam is released completely before opening the cover.

8. Use a food processor or blender to puree until smooth.

Creamy Corn Chowder (Clean eating, Gluten free, Dairy free, Vegan)

Preparation time: 15 minutes

Cooking time: 12 minutes

Servings: 6-8

Ingredients:

5 cups corn (from 6 ears of fresh corn)

4 tablespoons olive oil

1 medium onion, chopped

3 cups water

2 Idaho or Russet potatoes, diced

2 teaspoons dried thyme

1 teaspoon garlic powder

3 cups soy milk

1 /8 teaspoon cayenne pepper

2 cubes vegetable bouillon

2 tablespoons cornstarch, plus water for mixing

Salt and pepper, to taste

Directions:

1. Insert the inner pot into your Power Cooker, press the CHICKEN/MEAT button and add the olive oil. Sauté onion for 3 minutes.

2. Add 3 cups of water to the Power Cooker and insert the Steamer Tray. Place the corn and diced potatoes on the tray.

3. Cover the Power Cooker, lock the lid then turn the pressure release valve to closed.

4. Next, press the WARM/CANCEL button then choose the FISH/VEGETABLE button and adjust the time to 4 minutes.

5. When the time is up, the Power Cooker will switch to KEEP WARM automatically. Turn the pressure release valve to open.

6. Wait until the steam is released completely before opening the cover.

7. Carefully remove the Steamer Tray with corn and potato.

8. Add the corn and potato to the cooking liquid in the Power Cooker then stir in thyme, garlic powder, soy milk, cayenne pepper and vegetable bouillon.

6. Mix cornstarch with a little water in a bowl and stir it into the pot.

7. Press the CHICKEN/MEAT button and let simmer until the soup thickens. Season with salt and pepper.

POULTRY MAIN DISHES

Soft And Juicy Chicken (Clean eating, Gluten free, Paleo, Low carb, Dairy free)

Preparation time: 10 minutes

Cooking time: 35 minutes

Servings: 8

Ingredients:

1 whole (4 pound) chicken

1 tablespoon coconut oil

1 teaspoon dried thyme

1 teaspoon paprika

1/2 teaspoon sea salt

1/4 teaspoon freshly ground black pepper

2 tablespoon lemon juice

1 1/2 cups chicken broth

6 garlic cloves, peeled

Directions:

1. In a small bowl, mix together thyme, paprika, salt, and pepper. Rub the mixture all over the chicken.

2. Insert the inner pot into your Power Cooker, press the CHICKEN/MEAT button and add the coconut oil.

3. Cook the chicken in coconut oil until brown.

4. Add the lemon juice, broth and garlic cloves.

5. Cover the Power Cooker, lock the lid then turn the pressure release valve to closed.

6. Next, press the WARM/CANCEL button. Choose SOUP/STEW and press the COOK TIME button to 30 minutes.

7. When the time is up, the Power Cooker will switch to KEEP WARM automatically. Turn the pressure release valve to open.

8. Wait until the steam is released completely before opening the cover.

Barbecue Chicken Wings (Clean eating, Gluten free, Paleo, Low carb, Dairy free)

Preparation time: 10 minutes

Cooking time: 20 minutes

Servings: 6

Ingredients:

3 pounds chicken wings, cut, patted dry

Salt and pepper, to taste

2 garlic cloves, chopped

1/2 cup paleo barbecue sauce

1/4 cup honey mustard

3 lemon slices

1 1/2 tablespoons arrowroot powder

Directions:

1. Preheat your oven to Broil. Arrange chicken wings on a rack on a baking sheet. Sprinkle generously with salt and pepper. Broil on each side for 5 minutes.

2. Meanwhile, in a small bowl, mix together garlic, barbecue sauce and honey mustard.

3. Place the inner pot into the Power Cooker. Combine the chicken with the sauce in the pot. Top with the lemon slices.

4. Cover the Power Cooker, lock the lid then turn the pressure release valve to closed.

5. Next, press the WARM/CANCEL button then choose SOUP/STEW (10 minutes).

6. When the time is up, the Power Cooker will switch to KEEP WARM automatically. Turn the pressure release valve to open.

7. Wait until the steam is released completely before opening the cover.

8. Remove the chicken then press the CHICKEN/MEAT button. Whisk in the arrowroot starch until you have the desired thickness.

9. Serve chicken wings topped with the sauce.

Power Cooker Chicken And Black Bean Stew (Clean eating, Gluten free, Paleo, Low carb, Dairy free)

Fall-off-the-bone tender chicken with delicious black bean stew.

Preparation time: 15 minutes

Cooking time: 50 minutes

Servings: 4 - 6

Ingredients:

4 chicken legs, divided into thighs and drumsticks

1 tablespoon of vegetable oil

8 ounces of smoked sausage, sliced

1 medium onion, diced

2 teaspoons ground cumin

8 ounces dried black beans

2 (4-ounce) cans diced green chilies

4 cups low-sodium chicken broth

1/4 cup chopped cilantro

Kosher salt, to taste

Freshly ground black pepper, to taste

Lime wedges, for serving

Directions:

1. Insert the inner pot into your Power Cooker, press the CHICKEN/MEAT button. Add oil and heat until hot then add the sausage. Cook the sausage for about 2 minutes, or until just crisp around edges.

2. Sauté the onions for 3 minutes. Add the cumin and cook for about 30 seconds, or until fragrant.

3. Add the chicken, dried black beans, chilies and broth. Add salt and pepper to taste. Stir everything together.

4. Cover the Power Cooker, lock the lid then turn the pressure release valve to closed.

5. Next, press the WARM/CANCEL button then choose the SOUP/STEW button and adjust the time to 40 minutes.

6. When the time is up, the Power Cooker will switch to KEEP WARM automatically. Turn the pressure release valve to open.

7. Wait until the steam is released completely before opening the cover.

8. Use tongs to transfer the chicken to a bowl.

9. With the lid open, press CHICKEN/MEAT and heat the beans stew for about 5 minutes, or until reduced and thickened.

10. Shred the chicken and stir the meat into the stew. Season with salt and pepper to taste.

11. Stir in the cilantro then serve with lime wedges.

Chicken And Rice (Clean eating, Gluten free, Dairy free)

Preparation time: 10 minutes

Cooking time: 10 minutes

Servings: 4

Ingredients:

2 boneless, skinless chicken breasts, large cubed

2 tablespoon olive oil

Sea salt, to taste

Freshly ground black pepper, to taste

1 onion, diced

1 garlic, clove, minced

1 green pepper, seeded, diced

3 scallions chopped

1 teaspoon minced ginger

1 cup broccoli florets

1 bag frozen mixed vegetables

1 cup long grain white rice

1 3/4 cup chicken stock

Directions:

1. Rub salt and pepper all over the chicken.

2. Insert the inner pot into your Power Cooker and add olive oil.

3. Press the CHICKEN/MEAT button. Add chicken and vegetables then sauté for about 2-3 minutes.

4. Stir in the rice and all the other ingredients.

5. Cover the Power Cooker, lock the lid then turn the pressure release valve to closed.

6. Next, press the WARM/CANCEL button then choose the RICE/RISSOTO button (6 minutes).

7. When the time is up, the Power Cooker will switch to KEEP WARM automatically. Turn the pressure release valve to open.

8. Wait until the steam is released completely before opening the cover.

9. Serve.

Apple Cranberry Chicken With Cabbage (Clean eating, Gluten free, Paleo, Low carb, Dairy free)

Cook this one pot meal quickly in your Power Cooker.

Preparation time: 5 minutes

Cooking time: 20 minutes

Servings: 4

Ingredients:

1 small head cabbage, cored, shredded

2 pounds boneless, skinless chicken breasts or thighs

2 apples, cored, sliced

1/2 cup chicken broth

1 cup cranberries (fresh or frozen)

1 tablespoon apple cider vinegar

1 tablespoon maple syrup

1 teaspoon cinnamon

1 teaspoon ground ginger

1/2 teaspoon salt, or to taste

Directions:

1. Insert the inner pot into your Power Cooker then add all the ingredients.

2. Cover the Power Cooker, lock the lid then turn the pressure release valve to closed.

3. Next, press the CHICKEN/MEAT button and adjust the time to 20 minutes.

4. When the time is up, the Power Cooker will switch to KEEP WARM automatically. Turn the pressure release valve to open.

5. Wait until the steam is released completely before opening the cover.

6. Serve warm.

Honey And Orange Glazed Turkey Wings (Clean eating, Gluten free, Low carb, Dairy free)

Preparation time: 10 minutes

Cooking time: 40 minutes

Servings: 4

Ingredients:

4 turkey wings

2-3 tablespoons oil

Salt, to taste

Pepper, to taste

1 medium onion, sliced roughly

3 garlic cloves, minced

1 cup shelled walnuts

1/2 cup honey

1 bunch fresh thyme

1 cup fresh orange juice

Directions:

1. Insert the inner pot into your Power Cooker, press the CHICKEN/MEAT button and add the olive oil. Rub salt and pepper on turkey wings then brown in hot oil on both sides, about 2-3 minutes per side. Transfer the wings to a plate.

2. Add onions and garlic to the oil then let cook briefly. Return the turkey to the Power Cooker (it is better to stand the wings for even cooking). Add walnuts, honey, thyme and orange juice.

3. Cover the Power Cooker, lock the lid then turn the pressure release valve to closed.

4. Next, press the WARM/CANCEL button then choose the CHICKEN/MEAT button and adjust the time to 22 minutes.

5. When the time is up, the Power Cooker will switch to KEEP WARM automatically. Turn the pressure release valve to open.

6. Wait until the steam is released completely before opening the cover.

7. Remove the thyme bunch and transfer turkey wings to a sheet pan. Place under the broiler for just 5 minutes to caramelize.

5. Meanwhile, press CHICKEN/MEAT and heat the cooking liquid in the Power Cooker until reduced by half.

6. Pour the contents of the Power Cooker on the turkey wings and serve.

Lemon And Olive Chicken (Clean eating, Gluten free, Paleo, Low carb, Dairy free)

This scrumptious chicken dish is rich in herbs and spices.

Preparation time: 10 minutes

Cooking time: 25 minutes

Servings: 6-8

Ingredients:

8 bone-in, skin-on chicken thighs

1/2 cup dry white wine

1/2 cup of water

1 cup mixed Greek olives

1 fresh lemon, sliced for garnish

1 tablespoon fresh oregano leaves for garnish

For The Marinade:

2 garlic cloves, chopped

1/2 bunch parsley, finely chopped

1/2 teaspoon crushed fennel seeds

1 tablespoon rosemary, roughly chopped

4 tablespoons extra virgin olive oil

3 lemons, juiced

1 teaspoon sea salt

1/4 teaspoon pepper

Directions:

1. In a large bowl, combine garlic, parsley, fennel seeds, rosemary, olive oil, lemon juice, salt and pepper. Mix together very well.

2. Remove the skin from the chicken thighs then place in the marinade bowl. Mix to cover with marinade then cover with plastic wrap. Place in the refrigerator for 1-2 hours. After 1-2 hours, remove the chicken and reserve the marinade.

3. Insert the inner pot into your Power Cooker, press the CHICKEN/MEAT button and add about 2 tablespoons of olive oil. Working in batches, add the chicken and brown on all sides for about 5 minutes. Set browned chicken aside.

4. Return the chicken to the pot then add the reserved marinade and 1/2 cup of water.

5. Cover the Power Cooker, lock the lid then turn the pressure release valve to closed.

6. Next, press the WARM/CANCEL button then choose the SOUP/STEW button (10 minutes).

7. When the time is up, the Power Cooker will switch to KEEP WARM automatically. Turn the pressure release valve to open.

8. Wait until the steam is released completely before opening the cover.

9. Transfer the chicken pieces to a serving platter and cover tightly with foil.

7. Press the CHICKEN/MEAT button and heat the cooking liquid, uncovered until thick and syrupy.

8. Turn off the heat and return the chicken pieces to the Power Cooker. Stir and let simmer in the residual heat for a few minutes.

9. Serve, sprinkled with olives, fresh oregano and lemon wedges.

Shredded Chicken Breast (Clean eating, Gluten free, Paleo, Low carb, Dairy free)

Shredded chicken for salads, sandwiches and other quick dishes.

Preparation time: 10 minutes

Cooking time: 18 minutes

Servings:

Ingredients:

4-6 pounds boneless, skinless chicken breast

2 cups water

Salt and pepper to taste

Directions:

1. Insert the inner pot into your Power Cooker then add all the ingredients.

2. Cover the Power Cooker, lock the lid then turn the pressure release valve to closed.

3. Next, press the CHICKEN/MEAT button and adjust the time to 18 minutes.

4. When the time is up, the Power Cooker will switch to KEEP WARM automatically. Turn the pressure release valve to open.

5. Wait until the steam is released completely before opening the cover.

6. Remove the chicken and shred. Use immediately or add shredded chicken with some of the cooking liquid to plastic bags and refrigerate.

Turkey And Gravy (Clean eating, Gluten free, Paleo, Low carb, Dairy free)

Preparation time: 15 minutes

Cooking time: 45 minutes

Servings: 6

Ingredients:

4 pound bone-in turkey breast, cut up

2 tablespoons coconut or olive oil

Salt and pepper, to taste

1 medium onion, diced

2 garlic cloves, diced

1/2 cup unsweetened white grape juice

2 teaspoon Herbs of Provence

1 cup chicken broth

2 teaspoon lemon juice

1 tablespoon arrowroot flour

Directions:

1. Salt and pepper the turkey generously.

2. Insert the inner pot into your Power Cooker, press the CHICKEN/MEAT button and add the olive oil.

3. Add the turkey and brown on all sides, about 3 minutes per side. You may have to work in batches. Remove and set aside on a platter.

4. Drain off the fat, leaving just about 1 tablespoon in the Power Cooker. Add onion and cook for about 3 minutes. Add Herbs of Provence and garlic then cook for about 40 seconds.

5. Stir in the grape juice and scrape up any browned bits from the bottom of the pan. Stir in the chicken broth.

6. Cover the Power Cooker, lock the lid then turn the pressure release valve to closed.

7. Next, press the WARM/CANCEL button then choose the CHICKEN/MEAT button and adjust the time to 25 minutes.

8. When the time is up, the Power Cooker will switch to KEEP WARM automatically. Turn the pressure release valve to open.

9. Wait until the steam is released completely before opening the cover.

10. remove the turkey and place on a platter.

7. Stir in arrowroot flour and lemon juice then let simmer until thickened.

8. Serve turkey with the sauce.

Chicken, Black Beans And Rice (Clean eating, Gluten free)

Preparation time: 10 minutes

Cooking time: 12 minutes

Servings: 4

Ingredients:

6 boneless chicken thighs

2 tablespoons butter

1/2 medium onion, chopped

1 red pepper, deseeded, chopped

2 large ripe tomatoes, chopped

2 garlic cloves, minced

1 cup uncooked long grain rice

2 1/2 cups water

1 (15-ounce) can red kidney beans, drained, rinsed

Salt, to taste

1/2 teaspoon black pepper

Directions:

1. Insert the inner pot into your Power Cooker, press the CHICKEN/MEAT button and add the butter.

2. When butter melts, add the onions, red pepper and tomatoes then cook for 3-5 minutes. Add garlic and cook for just 30 seconds.

3. Add the chicken rice, water, salt and black pepper to taste.

4. Cover the Power Cooker, lock the lid then turn the pressure release valve to closed.

5. Next, press the WARM/CANCEL button then press the RICE/RISOTTO button to 6 minutes.

6. When the time is up, the Power Cooker will switch to KEEP WARM automatically. Turn the pressure release valve to open.

7. Wait until the steam is released completely before opening the cover.

8. Use a fork to fluff the rice then stir in the beans. If necessary, add more salt and pepper.

5. Serve, garnished with chopped coriander leaves.

Tex Mex Turkey Chili (Clean Eating, Gluten free, Dairy free)

Preparation time: 10 minutes

Cooking time: 20 minutes

Servings: 8

Ingredients:

2 tablespoons vegetable oil, or preferred frying oil

1 large onion, peeled, chopped

1 1/2 pounds of ground turkey

2 cups homemade Bloody Mary mix

2 (14-ounce) cans kidney beans, drained, rinsed

2 (14-ounce) cans diced tomatoes with green chilies

1 1/2 cups water

4 tablespoons chili powder, divided

Directions:

1. Insert the inner pot into your Power Cooker, press the CHICKEN/MEAT button and add the oil.

2. Add the onion and cook, until light golden, about 7 minutes.

3. Add the ground turkey. Cook until brown, stirring and breaking it up in the process.

4. Add the Bloody Mary then stir well and scrape up any browned bits from the bottom of the pot.

5. Stir in the beans, tomatoes, 2 tablespoons of chili powder and the water. Bring to boil.

6. Cover the Power Cooker, lock the lid then turn the pressure release valve to closed.

7. Next, press the WARM/CANCEL button then press the BEANS/LENTILS button to 5 minutes.

8. When the time is up, the Power Cooker will switch to KEEP WARM automatically. Turn the pressure release valve to open.

9. Wait until the steam is released completely before opening the cover.

10. Stir in 2 tablespoons of chili powder then let sit for about 5 minutes before serving. Serve with your desired side and garnish.

BEEF AND LAMB MAIN DISHES

Beef Bourguignon (Clean eating, Gluten free, Paleo, Low carb, Dairy free)

Tender and really delicious!

Preparation time: 25 minutes

Cooking time: 30 minutes

Servings: 6

Ingredients:

2 pounds round steak, cut into bite size pieces

3 slices of bacon, sliced into 1/2 inch pieces

1 large onion, chopped

2 tablespoons arrowroot flour

1/2 cup beef stock

1 cup of dry red wine

2 1/2 cups fresh mushrooms, quartered

2 carrots, sliced

1/4 teaspoon basil

2 garlic cloves, minced

Directions:

1. Insert the inner pot into your Power Cooker, press the CHICKEN/MEAT button. Add the bacon and fry until it renders its fat.

2. Add the onion and cook for about 2 minutes.

3. Add the meat and cook for about 5 minutes.

4. Add the flour and stir until thoroughly mixed.

5. Stir in the beef stock, wine and seasonings.

6. Cover the Power Cooker, lock the lid then turn the pressure release valve to closed.

7. Next, press the WARM/CANCEL button then choose the CHICKEN/MEAT button and adjust the time to 20 minutes.

8. When the time is up, the Power Cooker will switch to KEEP WARM automatically. Turn the pressure release valve to open.

9. Wait until the steam is released completely before opening the cover.

10. Add mushrooms and carrots. Again, cover the Power Cooker, lock the lid. Choose the BEANS/LENTILS button (5 minutes).

11. When the time is up, the Power Cooker will switch to KEEP WARM automatically. Turn the pressure release valve to open.

12. Serve.

Maple Glazed Smoked Brisket (Clean eating, Gluten free, Dairy free)

Preparation time: 15 minutes

Cooking time: 1 hour 20 minutes

Servings: 2-3

Ingredients:

1 1/2 pounds beef brisket

2 tablespoons maple sugar or coconut sugar

1/2 teaspoon smoked paprika

1 teaspoon onion powder

1 teaspoon mustard powder

2 teaspoon sea salt

1 teaspoon black pepper

Olive oil

1 tablespoon liquid smoke

2 cup bone broth

3 fresh thyme sprigs

Directions:

1. In a small bowl combine maple sugar, smoked paprika, onion powder, mustard powder, sea salt and pepper.

2. Generously coat the meat on all sides with the sticky mixture.

3. Insert the inner pot into your Power Cooker and press the CHICKEN/MEAT button.

4. Cover the bottom of the inner pot with a little olive oil and add the brisket. Brown the brisket on all sides.

64

5. Add the liquid smoke, broth and thyme. Use a spatula to scrape browned bits off the bottom.

6. Cover the Power Cooker, lock the lid then turn the pressure release valve to closed.

7. Next, press the WARM/CANCEL button then choose the CHICKEN/MEAT button and adjust the time to 50 minutes.

8. When the time is up, the Power Cooker will switch to KEEP WARM automatically. Turn the pressure release valve to open.

9. Wait until the steam is released completely before opening the cover.

10. Remove the brisket from the pot. Press the CHICKEN/MEAT button again and let the sauce reduce uncovered for about 10 minutes.

11. Slice the meat and serve it with your favorite vegetable and some of the cooking liquid.

Beef Short Ribs (Clean eating, Gluten free, Dairy free, Low carb)
Easy, fall-apart-tender ribs in a delicious sauce.

Preparation time: 30 minutes

Cooking time: 1 hour 15 minutes

Servings: 6

Ingredients:

2 tablespoons olive oil

1-inch fresh ginger, peeled, chopped finely

2 garlic cloves, peeled, crushed

1 pinch red pepper flakes

1/2 cup apple juice

2/3 cup salt-free beef stock

6 beef short ribs

1-2 tablespoons water

2 tablespoons cornstarch

Directions:

1. Insert the inner pot into your Power Cooker, press the CHICKEN/MEAT button and add the olive oil. Add ginger, garlic and red pepper flakes. Sauté for 2-3 minutes.

2. Stir in the apple juice and beef stock. Add the ribs and coat with the liquid in the Power Cooker.

3. Cover the Power Cooker, lock the lid then turn the pressure release valve to closed.

4. Next, press the WARM/CANCEL button then choose the CHICKEN/MEAT button and adjust the time to 55 minutes.

5. When the time is up, the Power Cooker will switch to KEEP WARM automatically. Turn the pressure release valve to open.

6. Wait until the steam is released completely before opening the cover.

7. Transfer the ribs to a sheet pan. Place in the broiler for about 5 minutes. This will give the ribs a rich dark brown color.

8. Meanwhile, mix cornstarch and water in a small container then stir into the cooking liquid in the Power Cooker. Boil the mixture until it thickens to your desire, then pour it over the ribs before you serve.

10. Serve with steamed rice or cauliflower rice.

Pot Roast And Tangy Gravy (Clean eating, Gluten free, Dairy free, Low carb)

Preparation time: 20 minutes

Cooking time: 50 minutes

Servings: 12

Ingredients:

3 pounds boneless chuck roast, trimmed

1 tablespoon olive oil

3 cups beef broth

1 teaspoon dried basil

1 large onion, sliced

3 garlic cloves, chopped

5 large carrots, cut into chunks

1 pound turnips, each cut into 8 wedges

4 large potatoes, peeled, cubed

2 bunches parsley leaves, chopped

1 teaspoon capers

Salt, to taste

Pepper, to taste

Directions:

1. Insert the inner pot into your Power Cooker, press the CHICKEN/MEAT button and add the olive oil. Salt and pepper the roast then brown on all sides for 5 minutes in hot oil.

2. Stir in the beef broth.

3. Cover the Power Cooker, lock the lid then turn the pressure release valve to closed.

4. Next, press the WARM/CANCEL button then choose the CHICKEN/MEAT button and adjust the time to 30 minutes.

5. When the time is up, the Power Cooker will switch to KEEP WARM automatically. Turn the pressure release valve to open.

6. Wait until the steam is released completely before opening the cover.

7. Add the basil, onion, garlic, carrots, turnips and potatoes. Season with salt and pepper.

8. Again, cover the Power Cooker, lock the lid then turn the pressure release valve to closed.

9. Next, press the SOUP/STEW button to 10 minutes.

10. When the time is up, the Power Cooker will switch to KEEP WARM automatically. Turn the pressure release valve to open.

11. Wait until the steam is released completely before opening the cover.

12. Transfer the roast to a platter, let cool then slice. Use a slotted spoon to transfer vegetables to the platter.

6. Add parsley and capers to the cooking liquid. Bring to a boil and let simmer until thickened. Serve the meat with vegetables and sauce.

Beef Roast And Mushrooms (Clean eating, Gluten-free, Paleo, Low-carb)

Preparation time: 5 minutes

Cooking time: 40 minutes

Servings: 6

Ingredients:

2 pounds beef roast

2 medium yellow onions, chopped

1 celery stalk, diced

1 carrot, diced

1 garlic clove, pressed

2 tablespoons chopped fresh chives

8 ounces mushrooms, sliced

1/2 cup red wine

3/4 cups water

Olive oil

2 tablespoons butter

Salt and pepper, to taste

Directions:

1. Season the meat with salt and pepper.

2. Insert the inner pot into your Power Cooker, press the CHICKEN/MEAT button then add the butter and 1 tablespoon olive oil.

3. When butter is melted, add the meat and brown on all sides. Set meat aside.

4. Add the onion, celery and carrots. Cook until vegetables are soft.

5. Stir in the garlic, chives, sliced mushrooms, wine and 3/4 cups of water. Return meat to the Power Cooker. Season with more salt and pepper.

6. Cover the Power Cooker, lock the lid then turn the pressure release valve to closed.

7. Next, press the WARM/CANCEL button then choose the CHICKEN/MEAT button and adjust the time to 24 minutes.

8. When the time is up, the Power Cooker will switch to KEEP WARM automatically. Turn the pressure release valve to open.

9. Wait until the steam is released completely before opening the cover.

10. Transfer the roast beef to a serving platter. If the cooking liquid is too thin, return the Power Cooker to heat, uncovered and reduce to desired thickness. Serve.

Meatballs And Sauce (Clean eating, Gluten free, Paleo, Low carb)

Preparation time: 25 minutes

Cooking time: 15 minutes

Servings: 4

Ingredients:

1 pound ground beef

8 ounces ground pork

1 small onion, minced

1/2 cup almond meal

1 large egg, beaten

1 tablespoon dried oregano

1 tablespoons dried thyme

1 tablespoon minced fresh basil leaves

1/2 teaspoon salt

1/4 cup ghee

3 tablespoons arrowroot flour

2 cups beef stock

2 cups water

1/2 cup coconut milk

Salt, to taste

Pepper, to taste

1 tablespoon chopped fresh parsley

Directions:

1. In a large bowl, add together the beef, pork, onion, almond meal, egg, oregano, thyme, basil and salt. Mix well.

2. Use your hands to roll into meatballs, about 3/4 to 1-inch size.

3. Insert the inner pot into your Power Cooker, press the CHICKEN/MEAT button then add ghee.

4. When ghee is melted, stir in the arrowroot flour then whisk in the beef stock, water and coconut milk. Bring the sauce to a simmer and season with salt and pepper.

5. Carefully add the meatballs to the sauce.

6. Cover the Power Cooker, lock the lid then turn the pressure release valve to closed.

7. Next, press the WARM/CANCEL button then choose the SOUP/STEW button (10 minutes).

8. When the time is up, the Power Cooker will switch to KEEP WARM automatically. Turn the pressure release valve to open.

9. Wait until the steam is released completely before opening the cover.

10. Taste for seasoning. If the sauce is too thin, let simmer until thick enough.

7. Serve over vegetable noodles and garnish with fresh parsley.

Classic Beef Stew (Clean eating, Gluten free, Low carb, Dairy free)

This is so delicious, there will be no leftovers.

Preparation time: 15 minutes

Cooking time: 20 minutes

Servings: 4

Ingredients:

1 1/2 pounds rump roast or stew beef, cubed

1 tablespoon olive oil

1 large onion, chopped

2 garlic cloves, minced

3 carrots, peeled and cut into 1-inch chunks

1/2 teaspoon dried thyme

3 celery stalks, cut into chunks

1 tomato, chopped

4 potatoes, cut into chunks

Salt, to taste

Black pepper, to taste

1 1/2 cups water

Directions:

1. Insert the inner pot into your Power Cooker, press the CHICKEN/MEAT button and add the olive oil. Add the meat and let brown on all sides. Add the onion and garlic then cook and stir for 2 minutes.

2. Add the carrots, thyme, celery, tomato, potatoes, salt, pepper and water.

3. Cover the Power Cooker, lock the lid then turn the pressure release valve to closed.

4. Next, press the WARM/CANCEL button then choose the SOUP/STEW button and adjust the time to 15 minutes.

5. When the time is up, the Power Cooker will switch to KEEP WARM automatically. Turn the pressure release valve to open.

6. Wait until the steam is released completely before opening the cover.

7. Serve.

Tex Mex Beef Stew (Clean eating, Gluten free, Paleo, Low carb, Dairy free)

Delicious when freshly cooked and tastes even better as a leftover.

Preparation time: 10 minutes

Cooking time: 40 minutes

Servings: 6

Ingredients:

2 pounds beef rump roast, cubed

Salt, to taste

Pepper, to taste

1 tablespoon olive oil

1 medium onion, chopped

3 garlic cloves, crushed

1 jalapeno, seeded, diced

1 teaspoon oregano

1 large tomato, diced

1 teaspoon dried thyme

2 tablespoons balsamic vinegar

2 cups chicken broth

2 large carrots, cut in 1-inch chunks

2 celery stalks, cut into large chunks

1/2 cup minced cilantro, to garnish

Directions:

1. In a large bowl, rub salt and pepper generously all over the beef cubes.

2. Insert the inner pot into your Power Cooker, press the CHICKEN/MEAT button and add the olive oil. Add the seasoned beef, and let sear on one side for 3 minutes before turning to sear on the other side. Remove beef to a plate.

3. Add the onion and cook for 2-3 minutes. Stir in the garlic, jalapeno, oregano, tomato and thyme then cook for 1 minute.

4. Add the vinegar, chicken broth and the browned meat. Add the carrots and celery.

5. Cover the Power Cooker, lock the lid then turn the pressure release valve to closed.

6. Next, press the WARM/CANCEL button then choose the SOUP/STEW button and adjust the time to 30 minutes.

7. When the time is up, the Power Cooker will switch to KEEP WARM automatically. Turn the pressure release valve to open.

8. Wait until the steam is released completely before opening the cover.

9. Taste for season and adjust as necessary. If you want the stew thicker, let it simmer on the "keep warm" mode for a few minutes.

10. Serve with minced cilantro.

BBQ Baby Back Ribs (Clean eating, Gluten free, Paleo, Low carb, Dairy free)

Tender and juicy baby back ribs in less than one hour in the Power Cooker.

Preparation time: 15 minutes

Cooking time: 50 minutes

Servings: 4

Ingredients:

3 pounds beef back ribs

2 teaspoons coarse salt

1 teaspoons black pepper

1 teaspoon cayenne pepper

1 teaspoon paprika

1/2 teaspoon ground cumin

1 teaspoon dried oregano

1/2 teaspoon onion powder

1 teaspoon garlic powder

2 tablespoons olive oil

1 cup of beef broth

12 ounces homemade barbeque sauce

Directions:

1. Cut up the ribs into serving sizes.

2. Mix together the spices and rub all over the ribs.

3. Insert the inner pot into your Power Cooker, press the CHICKEN/MEAT button and add the olive oil. Add the ribs and brown on all sides.

4. Pour in the beef broth.

5. Cover the Power Cooker, lock the lid then turn the pressure release valve to closed.

6. Next, press the WARM/CANCEL button then choose the SOUP/STEW button and adjust the time to 35 minutes.

7. When the time is up, the Power Cooker will switch to KEEP WARM automatically. Turn the pressure release valve to open.

8. Wait until the steam is released completely before opening the cover.

9. Remove the ribs from the pot. Add the barbeque sauce to the cooking liquid, press the CHICKEN/MEAT button and let simmer for about 10 minutes to thicken.

10. Serve ribs with sauce.

Yummy Pot Roast (Clean eating, Gluten free, Paleo, Low carb, Dairy free)

Easy pot roast with a finger-licking sauce.

Preparation time: 20 minutes

Cooking time: 55 minutes

Servings: 8

Ingredients:

3 pounds boneless chuck roast, trimmed

1/2 teaspoon kosher salt

1/4 teaspoon freshly ground black pepper

2 tablespoons olive oil

2 cups beef broth

2 tablespoons fish sauce

1 tablespoon red wine vinegar

2 garlic cloves, minced

1 large onion, sliced

1 tablespoons dried thyme

2 parsnips, peeled, cut into 1-inch pieces

3 large carrots, cut into 1-inch pieces

1 pounds red potatoes, cut into 1-inch pieces

Salt, to taste

Pepper, to taste

Directions:

1. Season the roasts all over with salt and pepper.

2. Insert the inner pot into your Power Cooker, press the CHICKEN/MEAT button and add the olive oil. Add the roast and brown on all sides, about 5 minutes.

3. Stir in beef broth, fish sauce and red wine vinegar.

4. Cover the Power Cooker, lock the lid then turn the pressure release valve to closed.

5. Next, press the WARM/CANCEL button then choose the CHICKEN/MEAT button and adjust the time to 40 minutes.

6. When the time is up, the Power Cooker will switch to KEEP WARM automatically. Turn the pressure release valve to open.

7. Wait until the steam is released completely before opening the cover.

8. Add the garlic, onion, thyme, parsnips, carrots and potatoes.

9. Again, cover the Power Cooker, lock the lid. Press the SOUP/STEW button (10 minutes).

10. When the time is up, the Power Cooker will switch to KEEP WARM automatically. Turn the pressure release valve to open.

11. Open the lid, taste for seasoning and adjust as necessary. Transfer the meat and vegetables to a serving platter.

Moroccan Lamb Stew (Clean eating, Gluten-free, Low-carb, Dairy free)
A savory and sweet dish with a unique blend of spices.

Preparation time: 10 minutes

Cooking time: 40 minutes

Servings: 6

Ingredients:

3 pounds boneless lamb shoulder, cubed

1/8 teaspoon ground cardamom

1 teaspoon ginger powder

1 teaspoon cumin powder

1 teaspoon turmeric powder

2 teaspoons paprika

1/4 teaspoon crumbled saffron threads

2 garlic cloves, smashed

Olive oil

2 onions, sliced roughly

1 cup vegetable stock

1 cinnamon stick

1 bay leaf

1 1/4 cups raisins

1 cup blanched almonds

3 tablespoon honey

Salt, to taste

1 teaspoon pepper

Directions:

1. In a small bowl, mix together cardamom, ginger powder, cumin powder, turmeric powder, garlic, paprika, saffron and enough olive oil to make a paste. Rub the paste all over the meat. Set aside.

2. Insert the inner pot into your Power Cooker, press the CHICKEN/MEAT button and add enough olive oil to cover the bottom of the pot.

3. When the oil is hot, add onions and cook until tender, about 3 minutes. Transfer the onions to a plate and set aside.

4. Add the lamb pieces and brown on all sides for about 10 minutes.

5. Add the vegetable stock, stirring to scrape up any browned bits. Return the onions to the pot then add cinnamon stick, and bay leaf.

6. Cover the Power Cooker, lock the lid then turn the pressure release valve to closed.

7. Next, press the WARM/CANCEL button then choose the SOUP/STEW button and adjust the time to 25 minutes.

8. When the time is up, the Power Cooker will switch to KEEP WARM automatically. Turn the pressure release valve to open.

9. Wait until the steam is released completely before opening the cover.

10. Add the raisins, almonds, salt to taste, pepper and honey.

11. Press the CHICKEN/MEAT button and let heat for about 5 minutes or until the liquid reduces as desired. Remove and discard the cinnamon stick and bay leaf.

12. Serve with toasted almonds. It goes well with steamed rice.

Braised Lamb Shanks (Clean eating, Gluten free, Paleo-friendly, Low carb, Dairy free)

This savory dish can be on your table in just 45 minutes.

Preparation time: 10 minutes

Cooking time: 45 minutes

Servings: 4

Ingredients:

4 lamb shanks

1/4 cup almond flour

2 tablespoons olive oil

1 large onion, chopped

1 garlic clove, crushed

3 large carrots, sliced thickly

1 teaspoon dried oregano

1 teaspoon grated lemon zest

2 tablespoons tomato paste

3/4 cup red wine

1/4 cup beef stock or water

Salt, to taste

Fresh ground black pepper, to taste

Directions:

1. Toss lamb shanks with almond flour to coat. Shake off excess flour.

2. Insert the inner pot into your Power Cooker, press the CHICKEN/MEAT button and add 1 tablespoon olive oil. Add the shanks and brown. Transfer to a plate and set aside.

3. Add the remaining oil to the Power Cooker. Add onions, garlic and carrots. Cook with occasional stirring for 5 minutes.

4. Stir in the oregano, lemon zest, tomato paste, red wine and beef stock. Bring to a boil.

5. Returned the browned lamb shanks to the Power Cooker. Stir to coat with sauce then season with salt and pepper to taste.

6. Cover the Power Cooker, lock the lid then turn the pressure release valve to closed.

7. Next, press the WARM/CANCEL button then choose the CHICKEN/MEAT button and adjust the time to 30 minutes.

8. When the time is up, the Power Cooker will switch to KEEP WARM automatically. Turn the pressure release valve to open.

9. Wait until the steam is released completely before opening the cover.

10. If the gravy is not thick enough, let simmer uncovered for a few minutes more.

Moroccan African Lamb Shanks (Clean eating, Gluten free, Paleo, Low carb, Dairy free)

Preparation time: 20 minutes

Cooking time: 55 minutes

Servings: 4

Ingredients:

4 lamb shanks

1 tablespoon olive oil

1 large onion, coarsely chopped

3 medium carrots

2 garlic cloves

1/2 cup pitted prunes, coarsely chopped

3 tomatoes peeled, quartered, plus juices

1 teaspoon dried thyme

1/2 teaspoon ground cinnamon

1 cup water

Salt, to taste

Freshly ground black pepper, to taste

1/4 cup packed fresh cilantro leaves

Directions:

1. Insert the inner pot into your Power Cooker, press the CHICKEN/MEAT button and add the olive oil. Working in batches, brown lamb shanks on all sides. Set aside in a bowl.

2. Add onions and carrots; cook and stir until tender, about 7-8 minutes. Add the garlic and cook for 30 seconds.

3. Stir in prunes, tomatoes with juices, thyme, cinnamon and water. Return the lamb shanks to the Power Cooker.

4. Cover the Power Cooker, lock the lid then turn the pressure release valve to closed.

5. Next, press the WARM/CANCEL button then choose the CHICKEN/MEAT button and adjust the time to 30 minutes.

6. When the time is up, the Power Cooker will switch to KEEP WARM automatically. Turn the pressure release valve to open.

7. Wait until the steam is released completely before opening the cover.

8. Serve, garnished with cilantro leaves.

Indian Lamb Curry (Clean eating, Gluten free, Paleo, Low carb)

Enjoy the rich traditional flavor of lamb in this classic Indian dish.

Preparation time: 10 minutes

Cooking time: 30 minutes

Servings: 6

Ingredients:

1 1/2 pounds boneless lamb, fat trimmed, cubed

3 tablespoons olive oil

1 green chili pepper, chopped

4 whole cloves

1 cinnamon stick, 2 inches long

1 black cardamon pod

2 bay leaves

2 medium onions, chopped finely

2 garlic cloves, minced

1 tablespoon grated fresh ginger

1 large tomato, diced

1 cup of water

1 1/2 teaspoons garam masala

1 teaspoon cayenne pepper

2 teaspoons coriander powder

1/2 teaspoon turmeric

Salt, to taste

1/3 cup coconut milk

1 tablespoon chopped parsley

Directions:

1. Insert the inner pot into your Power Cooker, press the CHICKEN/MEAT button and add the olive oil. Add chili pepper, cloves, cinnamon, cardamon and bay leaves. Cook and stir for 2-3 minutes.

2. Add the onions; cook and stir for 7-8 minutes. Add garlic and ginger; cook and stir for just 1 minute.

3. Add the lamb and stir until browned a little.

4. Stir in the tomato, water, garam masala, cayenne pepper, coriander, turmeric and salt.

5. Cover the Power Cooker, lock the lid then turn the pressure release valve to closed.

6. Next, press the WARM/CANCEL button then choose the SOUP/STEW button and adjust the time to 20 minutes.

7. When the time is up, the Power Cooker will switch to KEEP WARM automatically. Turn the pressure release valve to open.

8. Wait until the steam is released completely before opening the cover.

9. Pour in the coconut milk. Press the CHICKEN/MEAT button, bring to a boil and cook for about 5 minutes. Taste for seasoning and adjust as necessary.

10. Serve, garnished with parsley.

PORK MAIN DISHES

Pork Roast With Cauliflower Sauce (Clean eating, Gluten free, Paleo, Low carb)

Preparation time: 20 minutes

Cooking time: 1 hour 15 minutes

Servings: 6

Ingredients:

2 pounds pork roast (thaw if frozen)

4 cups chopped cauliflower

2 ribs celery

4 garlic cloves

1 medium onion, chopped

2 cups water

1 teaspoon sea salt

1/2 teaspoon black pepper

2 tablespoons coconut oil or ghee

8 ounces portabella mushrooms, sliced

Directions:

1. Insert the inner pot into your Power Cooker. Add the cauliflower, celery, garlic, onion and water.

2. Top with the pork roast then season with sea salt and pepper.

3. Cover the Power Cooker, lock the lid then turn the pressure release valve to closed.

4. Next, press the CHICKEN/MEAT button and adjust the time to 60 minutes.

5. When the time is up, the Power Cooker will switch to KEEP WARM automatically. Turn the pressure release valve to open.

6. Wait until the steam is released completely before opening the cover.

7. Transfer pork roast carefully into an oven proof dish. Bake in the oven at 400°F for 10-15 minutes.

8. Meanwhile, transfer the cooked vegetables and broth to a blender and process until smooth, set aside.

9. Add coconut oil and mushrooms to the Power Cooker and press the CHICKEN/MEAT button. Cook for 3-5 minutes.

10. Add the blended veggies and continue cooking until thickened.

11. Shred the pork and serve, topped with mushroom gravy.

Sweet And Tangy Pulled Pork (Clean eating, Gluten free, Paleo, Low carb, Dairy free)

This moist pull pork goes well with cauliflower rice.

Preparation time: 10 minutes

Cooking time: 1 hour 20 minutes

Servings: 6

Ingredients:

2 pounds boneless pork roast

1 tablespoon lard or coconut oil

1 1/4 cups bone broth

12 ounces cranberries (fresh or frozen)

91

2 tablespoons apple cider vinegar

2 tablespoons chopped fresh herbs (e.g. marjoram, oregano, sage)

1 tablespoon maple syrup

1/4 teaspoon garlic powder

1/8 teaspoon ground cloves

1/4 teaspoon cinnamon

Sea salt

Directions:

1. Insert the inner pot into your Power Cooker, press the CHICKEN/MEAT button and add the lard or coconut oil.

2. Season pork generously with salt then place in hot oil. Brown for about 2 minutes on each side.

3. Add broth, cranberries, vinegar, chopped fresh herbs, maple syrup, garlic powder, ground cloves and cinnamon to the pot.

4. Cover the Power Cooker, lock the lid then turn the pressure release valve to closed.

5. Next, press the WARM/CANCEL button then choose the CHICKEN/MEAT button and adjust the time to 60 minutes.

6. When the time is up, the Power Cooker will switch to KEEP WARM automatically. Turn the pressure release valve to open.

7. Wait until the steam is released completely before opening the cover.

8. Remove the pork and shred, using two forks. Return shredded pork to the pot. Stir, taste the sauce and add more salt if necessary.

9. Press the CHICKEN/MEAT button and let heat through for 15 minutes to increase the pork's moisture and flavor.

10. Serve with steamed vegetables.

Power Cooker Carnitas (Clean eating, Gluten free, Paleo, Low carb, Dairy free)

The Power Cooker seals in the flavor and makes the carnitas quick and easy.

Preparation time: 5 minutes

Cooking time: 50 minutes

Servings: 8

Ingredients:

2 1/2 pounds boneless pork shoulder roast, cut into 1-inch chunks

2 tablespoons olive oil

1/2 teaspoon chili powder

1 teaspoon ground cumin

2 teaspoons kosher salt

1/2 teaspoon black pepper

3 garlic cloves, crushed

1 onion, sliced

1 (3 inch) cinnamon stick

2 teaspoon dried oregano

1/2 cup fresh lime juice

1 1/2 cups fresh orange juice

Directions:

1. In a small bowl, mix together olive oil, chili powder, cumin, salt and pepper.

2. Add the spice mixture to the pork and toss.

3. Insert the inner pot into your Power Cooker, press the CHICKEN/MEAT button. Brown pork for a few minutes.

4. Stir in the rest of the ingredients.

5. Cover the Power Cooker, lock the lid then turn the pressure release valve to closed.

6. Next, press the WARM/CANCEL button then choose the CHICKEN/MEAT button and adjust the time to 30 minutes.

7. When the time is up, the Power Cooker will switch to KEEP WARM automatically. Turn the pressure release valve to open.

8. Wait until the steam is released completely before opening the cover.

9. Remove the pork and place on a baking sheet. Place it under the oven broiler for about 15 minute, occasionally stirring and basting with juice from the cooker.

10. Serve.

Pork Chops With Sauerkraut (Clean eating, Gluten free, Paleo, Low carb, Dairy free)

Preparation time: 10 minutes

Cooking time: 20 minutes

Servings: 4

Ingredients:

4 (1-inch) thick pork chops

2 tablespoons olive oil

1 stalk celery, chopped finely

1 onion, sliced thinly

2 garlic cloves, minced

1/2 pound sliced bacon

3 cups sauerkraut, well drained

2 tablespoons apple juice

1 1/2 cups chicken broth

1/2 teaspoon dried oregano

1 teaspoon dried sage

1/2 teaspoon ground mustard

1/4 teaspoon paprika

1 teaspoon dried thyme

Salt and freshly ground pepper, to taste

Directions:

1. Insert the inner pot into your Power Cooker, press the CHICKEN/MEAT button and add the olive oil. Brown pork chops in hot oil then drain.

2. Add the rest of the ingredients to the Power Cooker.

3. Cover the Power Cooker, lock the lid then turn the pressure release valve to closed.

4. Next, press the WARM/CANCEL button then choose the SOUP/STEW button and adjust the time to 12 minutes.

5. When the time is up, the Power Cooker will switch to KEEP WARM automatically. Turn the pressure release valve to open.

6. Wait until the steam is released completely before opening the cover.

7. Taste for seasoning and add more if necessary.

Pork Roast, Cauliflower And Mashed Potato (Clean eating, Gluten-free, Low-carb)

Onepot roast and mashed potatoes with fresh and dried herbs.

Preparation time: 10 minutes

Cooking time: 45 minutes

Servings: 4-6

Ingredients:

1/2 pound red potatoes, cubed

3 cups cauliflower florets

2 pounds of boneless pork loin, trimmed

2 tablespoons Dijon mustard

1 teaspoon dried thyme

1 tablespoon of olive oil

2 tablespoon fresh rosemary, minced

1 tablespoon white balsamic vinegar

3/4 cup water

1/2 of teaspoon salt

1/2 of teaspoon black pepper

Directions:

1. In a heat proof bowl (that can fit into the Power Cooker), combine the potato and cauliflower florets then set aside.

2. Brush mustard all over the roast and sprinkle with thyme.

3. Insert the inner pot into your Power Cooker, press the CHICKEN/MEAT button and add the olive oil. Brown the roast on all sides.

4. Add rosemary, water, vinegar, salt and pepper to the Power Cooker.

5. Next lower the heat proof bowl into the Power Cooker over the roast. If the bowl tilts, crumble a piece of tin foil and use it to support the base.

6. Cover the Power Cooker, lock the lid then turn the pressure release valve to closed.

7. Next, press the WARM/CANCEL button then choose the CHICKEN/MEAT button and adjust the time to 35 minutes.

8. When the time is up, the Power Cooker will switch to KEEP WARM automatically. Turn the pressure release valve to open.

9. Wait until the steam is released completely before opening the cover.

10. Remove the bowl then wipe the base and sides with paper towels. Mash the contents.

11. Transfer the roast to a platter and slice thinly. Drizzle with some of the cooking liquid. Serve.

Wine Braised Pork Loin (Clean eating, Gluten-free)

Preparation time: 5 minutes

Cooking time: 45 minutes

Servings: 6

Ingredients:

2 tablespoons olive oil

2 tablespoons butter

2 pounds pork loin, tied securely

1 teaspoon dried sage

1/2 teaspoon ground coriander

1 bay leaf

2 teaspoon salt

Freshly ground black pepper

1 1/2 cups red wine

1 cup beef stock

Water

Directions:

1. Insert the inner pot into your Power Cooker, press the CHICKEN/MEAT button and add the olive oil. Add the pork loin and brown on all sides.

2. Add bay leaf, sage, coriander, salt, pepper, wine and beef stock. Add enough water to cover the meat by half.

3. Cover the Power Cooker, lock the lid then turn the pressure release valve to closed.

4. Next, press the WARM/CANCEL button then choose the CHICKEN/MEAT button and adjust the time to 35 minutes.

5. When the time is up, the Power Cooker will switch to KEEP WARM automatically. Turn the pressure release valve to open.

6. Wait until the steam is released completely before opening the cover.

7. Transfer the meat to a serving platter and cover with foil. Remove the bay leaves and discard.

8. Let the sauce cool then scoop out the fat. Return to heat, press the CHICKEN/MEAT button and simmer uncovered until reduced.

9. Slice the roast as desired then pour some warm sauce on it.

Pork Roast With Mushroom And Cauliflower (Clean eating, Gluten free, Paleo, Low carb)

Preparation time: 20 minutes

Cooking time: 1 hour 15 minutes

Servings: 4-6

Ingredients:

2 pounds boneless pork roast

2 tablespoons ghee, or fat of choice

1/2 large onion, chopped

3 garlic cloves

1/2 cup white wine

2 cups chicken broth

1 large head cauliflower, cut into florets

1 teaspoon dried basil

8 ounces baby bella mushrooms, sliced

3 tablespoons chopped fresh parsley

Salt and pepper to taste

Directions:

1. Rub pork with all over with salt and pepper.

2. Insert the inner pot into your Power Cooker, press the CHICKEN/MEAT button and melt the fat.

3. Add pork roast and brown on all sides. Remove and set aside.

4. Stir in the chicken broth and wine. Scrape up browned bits from the bottom. Add the pork roast, cauliflower and dried basil.

5. Cover the Power Cooker, lock the lid then turn the pressure release valve to closed.

6. Next, press the WARM/CANCEL button then choose the CHICKEN/MEAT button and adjust the time to 60 minutes.

7. When the time is up, the Power Cooker will switch to KEEP WARM automatically. Turn the pressure release valve to open.

8. Wait until the steam is released completely before opening the cover.

9. Add the mushrooms. Press the CHICKEN/MEAT button, bring to a boil and cook for 3-4 minutes.

10. Check for seasoning and adjust as necessary. Stir in parsley and serve.

Pork Risotto With Fennel (Clean eating, Gluten free, Low carb)

An unusual risotto with great flavor.

Preparation time: 15 minutes

Cooking time: 25 minutes

Servings: 4

Ingredients:

1 pound sweet Italian sausage, casings removed, crumbled

2 tablespoons olive oil

1 teaspoon fennel seeds

1 medium fennel bulb, halved, cored, sliced, thinly

1 small onion, chopped finely

1 cup chopped red bell pepper

1 1/2 cups Arborio rice

3/4 cup dry white wine

5 cups chicken broth

1 tablespoon unsalted butter

1 tablespoon chopped fresh thyme leaves

1/2 cup freshly grated Parmesan

Directions:

1. Insert the inner pot into your Power Cooker, press the CHICKEN/MEAT button and add 1 tablespoon of olive oil. Add the sausage and fennel seeds; cook and stir for about 7 minutes. Remove and set aside in a bowl.

2. Add the remaining oil to the Power Cooker. Add the sliced fennel bulb, onion and bell pepper; cook and stir until tender, about 5 minutes.

3. Add the rice and wine. Cook with stirring until the liquid is almost completely absorbed then stir in the broth.

4. Cover the Power Cooker, lock the lid then turn the pressure release valve to closed.

5. Next, press the WARM/CANCEL button then choose the BEANS/LENTILS button and adjust the time to 9 minutes.

6. When the time is up, the Power Cooker will switch to KEEP WARM automatically. Turn the pressure release valve to open.

7. Wait until the steam is released completely before opening the cover.

8. Stir in the sausage and fennel seeds, butter, thyme and 3/4 of the cheese. Season to taste with salt and pepper.

6. Select "keep warm" and let simmer for 2-3 minutes.

7. Serve, sprinkled with the remaining parmesan.

Tender Pork Chops (Clean eating, Gluten free, Paleo, Low carb, Dairy free)

This versatile pork chops can be served with rolls, bread or steamed vegetables.

Preparation time: 10 minutes

Cooking time: 30 minutes

Servings: 4

Ingredients:

4 pork chops (bone-in or boneless)

2 tablespoon olive oil

1 small onion, diced

5 medium potatoes, diced

1 carrot, diced

1 cup vegetable broth

1 tablespoon coconut aminos

1 teaspoon lemon juice

1/3 teaspoon hot sauce

Salt, to taste

Pepper, to taste

Directions:

1. Insert the inner pot into your Power Cooker, press the CHICKEN/MEAT button and add the olive oil. Brown pork chops on all sides. Transfer to a bowl and season with salt and pepper.

2.Add onions and cook for 2 minutes.

3. Return the browned pork to the Power Cooker. Add the potatoes, carrots, vegetable broth, coconut aminos, lemon juice and hot sauce.

4. Cover the Power Cooker, lock the lid then turn the pressure release valve to closed.

5. Next, press the WARM/CANCEL button then choose the CHICKEN/MEAT button (15 minutes).

6. When the time is up, the Power Cooker will switch to KEEP WARM automatically. Turn the pressure release valve to open.

7. Wait until the steam is released completely before opening the cover.

8. Taste for seasoning and add more if needed. Serve.

No-fuss Braised Pork (Clean eating, Gluten free, Low carb, Dairy free)

An effortless recipe with rich flavor and aroma.

Preparation time: 10 minutes

Cooking time: 45 minutes

Servings: 6-8

Ingredients:

5 pounds pork butt, cubed

2 tablespoons olive oil

2 cups chicken stock

1 small onion, minced

4 garlic cloves, minced

2 teaspoons cayenne pepper

1 teaspoon paprika

2 cups red wine

1/2 cup lemon juice

2 cups chicken stock

Directions:

1. Insert the inner pot into your Power Cooker. Add pork, olive oil, onion, garlic, cayenne pepper and paprika. Mix well.

2. Add the wine, lemon juice and chicken stock. Don't let the liquid go beyond the maximum fill line.

3. Cover the Power Cooker, lock the lid then turn the pressure release valve to closed.

4. Next, press the CHICKEN/MEAT button and adjust the time to 45 minutes.

5. When the time is up, the Power Cooker will switch to KEEP WARM automatically. Turn the pressure release valve to open.

6. Wait until the steam is released completely before opening the cover.

7. Serve with mashed potatoes, rice or noodles.

Pork Loin And Vegetables (Clean eating, Gluten free, Paleo, Low carb, Dairy free)
Savory pork with your favorite crisp and fresh vegetables.

Preparation time: 15 minutes

Cooking time: 50 minutes

Servings: 4

Ingredients:

2 pounds boneless pork top loin

3 tablespoons garlic powder

2 tablespoons olive oil

1 cup of water

1 bay leaf

3 potatoes, cubed

3 carrots, sliced

1 onion, sliced

2 celery ribs, sliced

Salt, to taste

Pepper, to taste

Directions:

1. Using a sharp knife, cut short slits, about 2 inches apart on the pork loin. Rub garlic powder, salt and pepper all over the pork loin.

2. Insert the inner pot into your Power Cooker, press the CHICKEN/MEAT button and add the olive oil.

3. Add the pork loin and brown on all sides. Remove the meat to a plate and drain excess fat from the Power Cooker.

4. Add 1 cup of water to the Power Cooker then add the bay leaf and the pork loin.

5. Cover the Power Cooker, lock the lid then turn the pressure release valve to closed.

6. Next, press the WARM/CANCEL button then choose the CHICKEN/MEAT button and adjust the time to 35 minutes.

7. When the time is up, the Power Cooker will switch to KEEP WARM automatically. Turn the pressure release valve to open.

8. Wait until the steam is released completely before opening the cover.

9. Add the potatoes, carrots, onion and celery.

10. Again, cover the Power Cooker, lock the lid. Choose the RICE/RISOTTO button (6 minutes).

11. When the time is up, the Power Cooker will switch to KEEP WARM automatically. Turn the pressure release valve to open.

12. Let stand for 5 minutes then remove the meat and cut to serving sizes.

Barbecue Pork Spare Ribs (Clean eating, Gluten free, Paleo, Low carb)

Melt-in-your-mouth pork in a yummy barbecue sauce.

Preparation time: 15 minutes

Cooking time: 30 minutes

Servings: 4

Ingredients:

2 pounds pork spareribs, cut into serving pieces

1 teaspoon onion powder

1 teaspoon pepper

1 teaspoon cayenne pepper

1 tablespoon olive oil

1 cup of water or broth

3 tablespoons tomato paste

2 tablespoons apple cider vinegar

1 teaspoon coconut aminos

1/8 teaspoon lemon juice

Dash of hot sauce

2 teaspoons Dijon mustard

1 teaspoon celery seed

1 teaspoon liquid smoke (optional)

Directions:

1. In a large bowl, rub onion powder, pepper and cayenne pepper all over the spareribs.

2. Insert the inner pot into your Power Cooker, press the CHICKEN/MEAT button and add the olive oil. Brown ribs evenly on all sides. Drain any excess fat and return ribs to the Power Cooker.

3. Add the rest of the ingredients and stir to coat the meat.

4. Cover the Power Cooker, lock the lid then turn the pressure release valve to closed.

5. Next, press the WARM/CANCEL button then choose the CHICKEN/MEAT button and adjust the time to 20 minutes.

6. When the time is up, the Power Cooker will switch to KEEP WARM automatically. Turn the pressure release valve to open.

7. Wait until the steam is released completely before opening the cover.

SEAFOOD AND FISH MAIN DISHES

Spicy Coconut Fish Stew (Clean eating, Gluten free, Paleo, Low carb, Dairy free)

A delightfully tasty fish stew with a rich coconutty flavor.

Preparation time: 5 minutes

Cooking time: 12 minutes

Servings: 4

Ingredients:

1 1/2 pounds fish fillets, cut into chunks

Olive oil

2 garlic cloves, squeezed

2 medium onions, sliced into strips

2 medium orange bell peppers, chopped

1/8 teaspoon ginger powder

2 teaspoon ground cumin

1 tablespoon ground coriander

1 teaspoon of hot pepper flakes

1/2 teaspoon ground turmeric

1/2 teaspoon crushed fennel seeds

2 cups coconut milk

2 green chilies, sliced into strips

2 large tomatoes, seeded, chopped

2 teaspoons salt, or to taste

Juice from 1/2 lemon

Directions:

1. Insert the inner pot into your Power Cooker, press the CHICKEN/MEAT button and heat a swirl of olive oil.

2. Add the garlic, onion and bell peppers. Cook with constant stirring until onion is tender, about 3-4 minutes.

3. Add the ginger powder, cumin, coriander, pepper flakes, turmeric and fennel seeds. Cook for additional 2 minutes.

4. Stir in the coconut milk, scraping up any browned bits from the bottom of the Power Cooker.

5. Add the tomatoes, green chilies and fish pieces. Stir gently to coat fish with the sauce.

6. Cover the Power Cooker, lock the lid then turn the pressure release valve to closed.

7. Next, press the WARM/CANCEL button then choose the FISH/VEGETABLE button and adjust the time to 5 minutes.

8. When the time is up, the Power Cooker will switch to KEEP WARM automatically. Turn the pressure release valve to open.

9. Wait until the steam is released completely before opening the cover.

10. Add salt to taste and drizzle with lemon juice. Serve it alone or with steamed brown rice.

Quick And Easy New England Clam Chowder (Clean eating)

Preparation time: 5 minutes

Cooking time: 18 minutes

Servings: 4

Ingredients:

1/2 pound lean bacon, diced

1 onion, minced

1 (10-ounce) can chopped clams in juice, juices reserved

1 (8-ounce) bottle clam juice

Water

2 potatoes, diced

1 pinch, red pepper flakes

1/2 teaspoon ground thyme

1 bay leaf

1 cup cream

1 cup milk

1 tablespoon flour

1 tablespoon butter

Salt, to taste

Pepper, to taste

Directions:

1. Insert the inner pot into your Power Cooker, press the CHICKEN/MEAT button.

2. Add diced bacon and cook until golden. When the bacon renders its fat, add onion, salt and pepper then cook until onions are tender.

3. Add some water to the clam juice to make it up to 2 cups. Pour the clam juice into the Power Cooker then add diced potatoes, pepper flakes, thyme and bay leaf.

4. Cover the Power Cooker, lock the lid then turn the pressure release valve to closed.

5. Next, press the WARM/CANCEL button then choose the FISH/VEGETABLE button and adjust the time to 7 minutes.

6. When the time is up, the Power Cooker will switch to KEEP WARM automatically. Turn the pressure release valve to open.

7. Wait until the steam is released completely before opening the cover.

8. Remove bay leaf and discard.

9. In the meantime, make a roux by mixing butter and flour together in a skillet. Heat on low heat and stir until blended.

10. Stir the roux into the Power Cooker then stir in the clam meat, milk and cream.

11. Press the CHICKEN/MEAT button and let simmer, uncovered for about 4-5 minutes.

Shrimp Paella (Clean eating, Gluten free, Paleo, Low carb, Dairy free)

Preparation time: 10 minutes

Cooking time: 10 minutes

Servings: 4

Ingredients:

1 pounds frozen, raw, peeled large shrimp

1 1/2 cups white rice

3 tablespoons extra-virgin olive oil

1 medium yellow onion, chopped

3 garlic cloves, minced

1 red pepper, seeded, thinly sliced

1 teaspoon Spanish saffron

1 1/2 cups chicken stock

3 tablespoons tomato paste

1/4 teaspoon chili powder

Salt and pepper, to taste

1/3 cup chopped Italian parsley leaves

1 lemon, cut into wedges

Directions:

1. Insert the inner pot into your Power Cooker, press the CHICKEN/MEAT button and add the olive oil. Add onion, garlic, red pepper and saffron. Cook for about 5 minutes.

2. Stir in the rice, chicken stock, tomato paste, chili powder, salt and pepper. Place the shrimp on top.

3. Cover the Power Cooker, lock the lid then turn the pressure release valve to closed.

4. Next, press the WARM/CANCEL button then choose the FISH/VEGETABLE button and adjust the time to 5 minutes.

5. When the time is up, the Power Cooker will switch to KEEP WARM automatically. Turn the pressure release valve to open.

6. Wait until the steam is released completely before opening the cover.

7. Garnish with the lemon wedges and chopped parsley.

Halibut With Vegetable Soup (Clean eating, Gluten free)

Preparation time: 10 minutes

Cooking time: 15 minutes

Servings: 4

Ingredients:

4 (6-ounce) pieces frozen halibut fillet or other white fish

2 tablespoons ghee or coconut oil

1 small red onion, sliced thinly

1 teaspoon grated fresh ginger

5-6 medium potatoes, peeled, cubed

1 cup dry white wine

2 cups chicken broth

1 celery stalk, chopped

2 teaspoon chopped parsley

Salt and pepper, to taste

Directions:

1. Insert the inner pot into your Power Cooker, press the CHICKEN/MEAT button and melt ghee or coconut oil.

2. Add the onion then cook and stir for about 3 minutes.

3. Stir in the ginger, potatoes, white wine, chicken broth and celery then bring to a boil. Season to taste with salt and pepper.

4. Insert the Steamer Tray and place the fish on the tray.

5. Cover the Power Cooker, lock the lid then turn the pressure release valve to closed.

6. Next, press the WARM/CANCEL button then choose the FISH/VEGETABLE button and adjust the time to 6 minutes.

7. When the time is up, the Power Cooker will switch to KEEP WARM automatically. Turn the pressure release valve to open.

8. Wait until the steam is released completely before opening the cover.

9. Remove the Steamer Tray and the fish and place on a platter.

10. Use an immersion or regular blender to puree the soup partly so as to thicken.

11. Return the fish to the sauce and add parsley. Let simmer on "keep warm" mode for a few minutes before serving.

Yummy Fish Chowder (Clean eating, Gluten free)

This hearty chowder is filling and you can make it easily.

Preparation time: 15 minutes

Cooking time: 15 minutes

Servings: 4-6

Ingredients:

14 ounces fresh, skinless, boneless, salmon fillet

1 medium onion, chopped finely

1 large potato, peeled, cut into chunks

2 cups chicken broth

2 cups water

1/2 cup dry white wine

1 1/2 cups milk

1/2 teaspoon salt

1/2 teaspoon ground black pepper

2 cups light cream

Directions:

1. Insert the inner pot into your Power Cooker. Add the fish, onion, potato, chicken broth, water, wine and milk.

2. Cover the Power Cooker, lock the lid then turn the pressure release valve to closed.

3. Next, press the FISH/VEGETABLE button to 10 minutes.

4. When the time is up, the Power Cooker will switch to KEEP WARM automatically. Turn the pressure release valve to open.

5. Wait until the steam is released completely before opening the cover.

6. Season with salt and pepper.

7. Return to heat (press the CHICKEN/MEAT button), stir in the cream and let simmer until slightly thickened.

Cod With Peas (Clean eating, Gluten free, Low carb, Dairy free)

Tasty steamed fish infused with the flavor of mixed herbs.

Preparation time: 5 minutes

Cooking time: 10 minutes

Servings: 4

Ingredients:

4 (6-ounce) cod fillets, thawed

2 garlic cloves, minced

4 scallions, white and green parts, chopped

1/2 teaspoon dried basil

1/2 teaspoon dried oregano

1/2 teaspoon paprika

10 ounces frozen peas

1 cup chicken broth

1/3 cup wine

Salt

Directions:

1. In a small bowl, add together garlic, scallions, basil, oregano and paprika.

2. Insert the inner pot into your Power Cooker then add the broth and wine together with the herb mixture. Season with salt and stir thoroughly.

3. Insert the Steamer Tray and place the fish on the tray.

4. Cover the Power Cooker, lock the lid then turn the pressure release valve to closed.

5. Next, press the FISH/VEGETABLE button and adjust the time to 3 minutes.

6. When the time is up, the Power Cooker will switch to KEEP WARM automatically. Turn the pressure release valve to open.

7. Wait until the steam is released completely before opening the cover.

8. Remove the fish and set aside.

5. Add the peas to the cooking liquid, press the CHICKEN/MEAT button, bring to a boil and cook, uncovered for 3-5 minutes.

6. Serve fish with peas.

Steamed Fish With Fresh Herb Sauce (Clean eating, Gluten free, Paleo, Low carb, Dairy free)

Preparation time: 10 minutes

Cooking time: 8 minutes

Servings: 4

Ingredients:

4 white fish fillets (cod or halibut)

Extra virgin olive oil

Salt, to taste

Pepper, to taste

1/2 teaspoon garlic powder

1 cup fish stock

1/4 cup arugula leaves, finely chopped

1/4 cup parsley, finely chopped

1 tablespoon oregano, finely chopped

1 tablespoon marjoram, finely chopped

2 teaspoons red wine vinegar

1 garlic clove, minced

Directions:

1. Pat fish fillets dry with a paper towel.

2. Rub olive oil on the fillets then season lightly with salt and pepper

3. Insert the inner pot into your Power Cooker then add the garlic powder and fish stock.

4. Insert the Steamer Tray and place the fish on the tray.

5. Cover the Power Cooker, lock the lid then turn the pressure release valve to closed.

6. Next, press the FISH/VEGETABLE button and adjust the time to 5 minutes.

7. When the time is up, the Power Cooker will switch to KEEP WARM automatically. Turn the pressure release valve to open.

8. Wait until the steam is released completely before opening the cover.

9. Meanwhile, in a medium bowl, combine 3 tablespoons olive oil, arugula, parsley, oregano, marjoram, minced garlic and vinegar. Season with a little salt and pepper then toss well.

7. Serve fish with fresh herb sauce.

Easy Steamed Fish (Paleo, Gluten free)
This easy steamed fish recipe produces a surprisingly pleasing result.

Preparation time: 5 minutes

Cooking time: 8 minutes

Servings: 4

Ingredients:

4 white fish fillets (cod etc)

1 pound cherry tomatoes, sliced

1 bunch of fresh thyme, a few sprigs reserved

1 garlic clove, crushed

Olive oil

2 tablespoon pickled capers

1 cup olives

Salt and pepper, to taste

Directions:

1. In a heatproof bowl (that can fit in the Power Cooker), layer cherry tomatoes and fresh thyme. Next layer fish then add crushed garlic, salt and olive oil.

2. Insert the inner pot into your Power Cooker then place the heatproof bowl inside.

3. Cover the Power Cooker, lock the lid then turn the pressure release valve to closed.

4. Next, press the FISH/VEGETABLE button and adjust the time to 5 minutes.

5. When the time is up, the Power Cooker will switch to KEEP WARM automatically. Turn the pressure release valve to open.

6. Wait until the steam is released completely before opening the cover.

7. Serve fillets in separate plates, sprinkle with pepper, more thyme, olives, capers and drizzle with olive oil.

RICE AND PASTA RECIPES

Sausage Risotto (Clean eating, Gluten free)

Preparation time: 15 minutes

Cooking time: 15 minutes

Servings: 6

Ingredients:

2 pounds rope sausage, sliced

4 tablespoons butter

1 tablespoon Cajun seasoning

1 teaspoon sea salt

2 medium onions, diced

3 1/2 cups broth

2 cups arborio rice

2 small summer squash, seeded, diced

1 1/2 cups bell peppers, diced

1/2 cup fresh cilantro, chopped

Directions:

1. Sprinkle the sausage with Cajun seasoning and sea salt.

2. Insert the inner pot into your Power Cooker, press the CHICKEN/MEAT button and add the butter.

3. When butter is melted, add the sausage. Cook with constant stirring until browned, about 3 minutes.

4. Add onions; cook and stir until softened, about 3-4 minutes.

5. Stir in broth and bring to a boil.

6. Add the rice, summer squash and bell peppers. Stir to combine.

7. Cover the Power Cooker, lock the lid then turn the pressure release valve to closed.

8. Next, press the WARM/CANCEL button then choose the BEANS/LENTILS button (5 minutes).

9. When the time is up, the Power Cooker will switch to KEEP WARM automatically. Turn the pressure release valve to open.

10. Wait until the steam is released completely before opening the cover.

11. Stir and serve, topped with chopped cilantro.

Rice Pilaf With Veggies (Clean eating, Gluten free, Dairy free, Vegan)

Preparation time: 5 minutes

Cooking time: 12 minutes

Servings: 4

Ingredients:

2 tablespoon oil

1 onion, diced

1 cup long grain white rice

2 cups vegetable stock

1/2 teaspoon ground cinnamon

1 carrot, chopped

1 teaspoon salt

2 tablespoon frozen peas

1 tablespoon fresh parsley, chopped

Directions:

1. Insert the inner pot into your Power Cooker, press the CHICKEN/MEAT button and add the olive oil. Add the onions; cook and stir for about 5 minutes.

2. Add the uncooked rice; cook and stir for 1-2 minutes. Stir in the vegetable stock, cinnamon, carrot, salt and peas.

3. Cover the Power Cooker, lock the lid then turn the pressure release valve to closed.

4. Next, press the WARM/CANCEL button then choose the FISH/VEGETABLE button and adjust the time to 5 minutes.

5. When the time is up, the Power Cooker will switch to KEEP WARM automatically. Turn the pressure release valve to open.

6. Wait until the steam is released completely before opening the cover.

7. Open the lid, fluff rice with a fork, stir in parsley then serve.

Zesty Penne With Sausage (Clean eating, Gluten free)

Preparation time: 15 minutes

Cooking time: 25 minutes

Servings: 4-6

Ingredients:

1 pound gluten free Italian Sausage

1 tablespoon olive oil

1 large onion, chopped

2 garlic cloves, minced

1/2 teaspoon red pepper flakes

2 teaspoons dried parsley

2 teaspoons oregano

2 (14.5-ounce) cans tomato sauce

1 cup water

4 cups gluten free penne, cooked and drained

Salt and pepper, to taste

1/2 cup Parmesan Cheese, grated

Directions:

1. Insert the inner pot into your Power Cooker, press the CHICKEN/MEAT button and add the olive oil. Add the onion and cook for 5 minutes. Add the garlic and cook for 1 minute.

2. Add the sausage. Cook and stir, breaking up the sausage, about 6 minutes.

3. Add the pepper flakes, dried parsley, oregano, tomato sauce and water.

4. Cover the Power Cooker, lock the lid then turn the pressure release valve to closed.

5. Next, press the WARM/CANCEL button then choose the RICE/RISOTTO button and adjust the time to 7 minutes.

6. When the time is up, the Power Cooker will switch to KEEP WARM automatically. Turn the pressure release valve to open.

7. Wait until the steam is released completely before opening the cover.

8. Stir in the cooked pasta then add salt and pepper to taste. Press the CHICKEN/MEAT button and let simmer uncovered for 4-5 minutes.

6. Serve, sprinkled with grated cheese.

Creamy White Wine Risotto (Clean eating, Gluten free)

Preparation time: 5 minutes

Cooking time: 15 minutes

Servings: 4-6

Ingredients:

2 tablespoons butter

1 1/2 cups Carnaroli or Arborio rice

1 medium onion, chopped finely

2 garlic cloves, minced

1 cup dry white wine

3 cups vegetable broth

Salt, to taste

Pepper, to taste

3/4 cup grated Parmesan cheese

Directions:

1. Insert the inner pot into your Power Cooker, press the CHICKEN/MEAT button and add the butter.

2. When butter melts, sauté the onion for about 3 minutes. Add garlic then cook and stir for 30 seconds more.

3. Stir in the rice; cook and stir for 2 minutes.

4. Add the wine, cook and stir until absorbed. Stir in the broth.

5. Cover the Power Cooker, lock the lid then turn the pressure release valve to closed.

6. Next, press the WARM/CANCEL button then choose the RICE/RISOTTO button and adjust the time to 10 minutes.

7. When the time is up, the Power Cooker will switch to KEEP WARM automatically. Turn the pressure release valve to open.

8. Wait until the steam is released completely before opening the cover.

9. Stir in the grated Parmesan and season with salt and pepper. Stir until cheese melts.

6. Serve hot.

Mushroom And Asparagus Risotto (Clean eating, Gluten free, Paleo, Dairy free, Vegan)

Preparation time: 10 minutes

Cooking time: 15 minutes

Servings: 4

Ingredients:

1 pound asparagus, trimmed, cut into 1-inch pieces

4 cups vegetable broth

2 tablespoons olive oil

1 medium onion, chopped

3 cups sliced mushrooms

2 teaspoons salt

Fresh-ground black pepper

2 cups arborio rice

1/4 cup dry white wine

1/2 teaspoon grated lemon zest

Extra-virgin olive oil or grated vegan Parmesan for garnish

Directions:

1. Insert the inner pot into your Power Cooker, press the CHICKEN/MEAT button and add the broth and asparagus.

2. Cover the Power Cooker, lock the lid then turn the pressure release valve to closed.

3. Next, press the FISH/VEGETABLE button (2 minutes).

4. When the time is up, the Power Cooker will switch to KEEP WARM automatically. Turn the pressure release valve to open.

5. Wait until the steam is released completely before opening the cover.

6. Pour the contents of the Power Cooker into a bowl.

7. Press the CHICKEN/MEAT button and heat the olive oil. Add onion and sauté for 2 minutes. Add the mushroom, season with salt and pepper then cook with constant stirring for 3 minutes.

8. Add the rice and cook with constant stirring for 2 minutes. Add the wine and cook until almost completely evaporated.

9. Return the asparagus and broth to the Power Cooker. Mix well, scraping up any stuck bits from the bottom of the pan.

10. Again, cover the Power Cooker, lock the lid then turn the pressure release valve to closed.

11. Next, press the WARM/CANCEL button then choose the RICE/RISOTTO button (6 minutes).

12. When the time is up, the Power Cooker will switch to KEEP WARM automatically. Turn the pressure release valve to open.

13. Wait until the steam is released completely before opening the cover.

14. Stir in the lemon zest and let heat through in the residual heat. Serve with a swirl of extra-virgin olive oil or sprinkle with grated vegan Parmesan.

Turkey Rice Pilaf (Clean eating, Gluten free)

Preparation time: 5 minutes

Cooking time: 15 minutes

Servings: 4

Ingredients:

1/2 pound cooked turkey breast, cut into bite size pieces

2 tablespoons olive oil

1 cup sliced celery

1 onion, chopped

1 cup long grain white rice

2 cups chicken broth

1 large carrot, chopped

1 bay leaf

1/2 teaspoon salt

2 tablespoon fresh parsley, chopped (optional)

Directions:

1. Insert the inner pot into your Power Cooker, press the CHICKEN/MEAT button and add the olive oil. Add onion and celery; cook with occasional stirring, about 5 minutes.

2. Add the uncooked rice; cook and stir for 1-2 minutes. Stir in the chicken broth, carrot, bay leaf and salt.

3. Cover the Power Cooker, lock the lid then turn the pressure release valve to closed.

4. Next, press the WARM/CANCEL button then choose the BEANS/LENTILS button (5 minutes).

5. When the time is up, the Power Cooker will switch to KEEP WARM automatically. Turn the pressure release valve to open.

6. Wait until the steam is released completely before opening the cover.

7. Remove the bay leaf and discard.

5. Stir in the turkey breast. Press the CHICKEN/MEAT button and cook, uncovered, for about 2 to 3 minutes (if most of the liquid has been absorbed, add a little chicken broth).

6. Fluff rice with a fork, stir in parsley then serve.

Lentil Vegetable Risotto (Clean eating, Gluten free, Dairy free, Vegan)

Preparation time: 5 minutes

Cooking time: 15 minutes

Servings: 6

Ingredients:

1 1/2 tablespoons olive oil

10-12 sage leaves

1/2 yellow onion, diced

2 garlic cloves, minced

2 small carrots grated

1/2 jalapeno, seeded, diced

1 cup dry lentils (brown or green), soaked overnight

1 1/2 cups arborio rice

4 cups vegetable stock

1 teaspoon salt

Directions:

1. Insert the inner pot into your Power Cooker, press the CHICKEN/MEAT button and add some olive oil. Add the sage leaves and stir fry for 1 minute. Set aside in a plate.

2. Add the rest of the oil then sauté the onion, garlic, carrots and jalapeno until just soften.

3. Add the rice and cook with constant stirring for 1 minute.

4. Stir in the lentils, vegetable stock and salt.

5. Cover the Power Cooker, lock the lid then turn the pressure release valve to closed.

6. Next, press the WARM/CANCEL button then choose the RICE/RISOTTO button and adjust the time to 7 minutes.

7. When the time is up, the Power Cooker will switch to KEEP WARM automatically. Turn the pressure release valve to open.

8. Wait until the steam is released completely before opening the cover.

9. Serve, garnished with sage leaves and drizzled with extra virgin olive oil.

Spaghetti Bolognaise (Clean eating, Gluten free)

Preparation time: 15 minutes

Cooking time: 30 minutes

Servings: 6

Ingredients:

1 pound lean ground beef

2 tablespoons olive oil

1 large onion, chopped finely

3 garlic cloves, minced

2 celery sticks, sliced

2 carrots, chopped finely

1 1/2 cups beef stock

2 (14.5-ounce) cans chopped tomatoes

2 tablespoons tomato paste

1/2 teaspoon dried basil

1 teaspoon dried oregano

Salt, to taste

Freshly ground black pepper, to taste

2-3 tablespoons freshly grated Parmesan cheese

1 pound spaghetti, cooked

Directions:

1. Insert the inner pot into your Power Cooker, press the CHICKEN/MEAT button and add the olive oil.

2. Add onion and stir fry for 3 minutes. Add garlic and cook for just 30 seconds. Add the celery and carrots then cook for additional 5 minutes.

3. Stir in ground beef and cook until no longer pink.

4. Stir in the beef stock, chopped tomatoes, tomato paste, basil, oregano, salt and pepper.

5. Cover the Power Cooker, lock the lid then turn the pressure release valve to closed.

6. Next, press the WARM/CANCEL button then choose the RICE/RISOTTO button and adjust the time to 15 minutes.

7. When the time is up, the Power Cooker will switch to KEEP WARM automatically. Turn the pressure release valve to open.

8. Wait until the steam is released completely before opening the cover.

9. Meanwhile, cook the spaghetti according to package directions.

10. Serve spaghetti with the sauce and pass cheese at the table.

Mexican Rice (Clean eating, Gluten free, Dairy free, Vegan)

Preparation time: 5 minutes

Cooking time: 5 minutes

Servings: 6

Ingredients:

1 cup rice long grain rice

2 1/4 cups vegetable broth

1 cup chopped tomatoes plus juice

2 tablespoons vegan butter

1 medium onion, finely diced

1 garlic clove, minced

1 teaspoon oregano

1/8 teaspoon cayenne pepper

1 tablespoon fresh parsley, chopped

Salt, to taste

Directions:

1. Insert the inner pot into your Power Cooker. Add all the ingredients and mix well.

2. Cover the Power Cooker, lock the lid then turn the pressure release valve to closed.

3. Next, press the BEANS/LENTILS button (5 minutes).

139

4. When the time is up, the Power Cooker will switch to KEEP WARM automatically. Turn the pressure release valve to open.

5. Wait until the steam is released completely before opening the cover.

6. Let sit for about 5 minutes then stir and serve.

VEGETABLE MAIN DISHES

Spaghetti Squash And Pesto (Clean eating, Gluten-free, Vegetarian)

A simple meal that everyone will enjoy.

Preparation time: 5 minutes

Cooking time: 8 minutes

Servings: 4

Ingredients:

1 medium spaghetti squash

1 cup water

Toppings: Pesto sauce, Cheese

Directions:

1. Cut the ends of the squash then cut it in half crosswise. Use a spoon to scoop out the seeds.

2. Insert the inner pot into your Power Cooker then add 1 cup of water and the squash.

3. Cover the Power Cooker, lock the lid then turn the pressure release valve to closed.

4. Next, press the FISH/VEGETABLE button and adjust the time to 8 minutes.

5. When the time is up, the Power Cooker will switch to KEEP WARM automatically. Turn the pressure release valve to open.

6. Wait until the steam is released completely before opening the cover.

7. Remove the squash from the Power Cooker. Using a fork, carefully remove the squash fibers from the shell and place on a platter.

5. Serve, topped with pesto sauce and garnished with a sprinkle of cheese.

German Potato Salad (Clean eating, Gluten free, Dairy free, Vegan)

Classic German potato salad (sans bacon) made quickly in the Power Cooker.

Preparation time: 15 minutes

Cooking time: 5 minutes

Servings: 4-6

Ingredients:

2 pounds potatoes, sliced into 1/2-inch pieces

1 onion, chopped finely

1/3 cup cider vinegar

1/3 cup water

1/2 teaspoon celery seed

1 teaspoon whole grain mustard

1 tablespoon sugar

2 tablespoons minced fresh parsley

Salt and pepper, to taste

Directions:

1. Insert the inner pot into your Power Cooker then add potato and onions.

2. In a bowl, combine the rest of the ingredients. Pour the mixture over the potato and onions.

3. Cover the Power Cooker, lock the lid then turn the pressure release valve to closed.

4. Next, press the BEANS/LENTILS button (5 minutes).

5. When the time is up, the Power Cooker will switch to KEEP WARM automatically. Turn the pressure release valve to open.

6. Wait until the steam is released completely before opening the cover.

7. Taste and adjust seasoning as needed. Serve warm or refrigerate to serve cold.

Zucchini And Cherry Tomato (Gluten free, Paleo, Low carb, Dairy free, Vegan)

Easy to cook and really satisfying.

Preparation time: 3 minutes

Cooking time: 15 minutes

Servings: 4

Ingredients:

1 tablespoon of olive oil

1 onion, chopped roughly

1 pound cherry tomatoes

4 medium zucchini, chopped

2 tablespoons tomato paste

3/4 cup water

1/2 teaspoon dried basil

1/2 teaspoon dried oregano

1 teaspoon salt

2 garlic cloves, minced finely

1 bunch of basil

Extra-virgin olive oil

Directions:

1. Insert the inner pot into your Power Cooker, press the CHICKEN/MEAT button and add the olive oil. Add the onion and cook until tender, about 5 minutes.

2. Stir in cherry tomatoes, chopped zucchini, tomato paste, water, basil, oregano and salt.

3. Cover the Power Cooker, lock the lid then turn the pressure release valve to closed.

4. Next, press the WARM/CANCEL button then choose the FISH/VEGETABLE button and adjust the time to 6 minutes.

5. When the time is up, the Power Cooker will switch to KEEP WARM automatically. Turn the pressure release valve to open.

6. Wait until the steam is released completely before opening the cover.

7. Stir in the garlic then use a slotted spoon to strain out the veggies and serve with fresh basil and a drizzle of olive oil.

Note: You can refrigerate the cooking liquid and use as stock for another recipe.

Spicy Vegetable Curry (Clean eating, Gluten free, Low carb, Dairy free, Vegan)

Preparation time: 20 minutes

Cooking time: 10 minutes

Servings: 6

Ingredients:

1 tablespoon olive oil

1 yellow onion, diced

4 potatoes, peeled, cubed

1 bell pepper

1 serrano pepper, diced

6 tablespoons mild curry paste

1/2 cup water

1/2 cup coconut milk

1 (15-ounce) can peas, drained

1 (15-ounce) can chickpeas (garbanzo beans), rinsed, drained

1 tablespoon chopped fresh parsley

Salt and pepper, to taste

Directions:

1. Insert the inner pot into your Power Cooker, press the CHICKEN/MEAT button and add the olive oil. Add the onions; cook and stir for about 5 minutes.

2. Add the potatoes, bell pepper, serrano pepper, curry paste, water and coconut milk. Season to taste with salt and pepper.

3. Cover the Power Cooker, lock the lid then turn the pressure release valve to closed.

4. Next, press the WARM/CANCEL button then choose the FISH/VEGETABLE button and adjust the time to 4 minutes.

5. When the time is up, the Power Cooker will switch to KEEP WARM automatically. Turn the pressure release valve to open.

6. Wait until the steam is released completely before opening the cover.

7. Stir in the peas and chickpeas.

8. Serve, garnished with parsley.

Red Cabbage Salad (Clean eating, Gluten free, Paleo, Low carb, Dairy free, Vegan)

The cabbage will provide enough liquid to cook itself in the Power Cooker.

Preparation time: 15 minutes

Cooking time: 3 minutes

Servings: 6

Ingredients:

1 head red cabbage, sliced thinly

1 onion, chopped

1 tablespoon extra-virgin olive oil

1 gala or red delicious apple, diced

1/4 cup raisins

1/4 cup apple cider vinegar

Salt and pepper, to taste

Directions:

1. Insert the inner pot into your Power Cooker and add all the ingredients.

2. Cover the Power Cooker, lock the lid then turn the pressure release valve to closed.

3. Next, press the FISH/VEGETABLE button and adjust the time to 3 minutes.

4. When the time is up, the Power Cooker will switch to KEEP WARM automatically. Turn the pressure release valve to open.

5. Wait until the steam is released completely before opening the cover.

6. Stir, taste and add more seasoning if necessary.

Summer Mixed Vegetables (Clean eating, Gluten free, Dairy free, Vegetarian)

Preparation time: 15 minutes

Cooking time: 12 minutes

Servings: 6

Ingredients:

1/4 cup olive oil

2 medium potatoes, cubed

1 medium sweet onion, sliced

1 bell pepper, sliced

2 medium zucchini, cut into 1/4-inch slices

1 medium yellow summer squash, cut into 1/4-inch slices

2 medium carrots, sliced

10 large fresh mushrooms

1 1/2 teaspoons minced fresh parsley

1 1/2 teaspoons minced fresh basil

1 1/2 teaspoons minced fresh chives

1/4 cup water

10 cherry tomatoes, halved

Salt, to taste

Pepper, to taste

Directions:

1. Wash all the vegetables and slice.

2. Insert the inner pot into your Power Cooker, press the CHICKEN/MEAT button and add the olive oil.

3. Add the potatoes and cook with constant stirring for 3 minutes. Add the onion and bell pepper, continue cooking and stirring for 3 minutes more.

4. Add zucchini, summer squash, carrots and mushrooms then cook and stir for additional 3 minutes.

5. Next, add the minced parsley, basil, chives and water. Season to taste with salt and pepper.

6. Cover the Power Cooker, lock the lid then turn the pressure release valve to closed.

7. Next, press the WARM/CANCEL button then choose the FISH/VEGETABLE button and adjust the time to 5 minutes.

8. When the time is up, the Power Cooker will switch to KEEP WARM automatically. Turn the pressure release valve to open.

9. Wait until the steam is released completely before opening the cover.

10. Immediately transfer all the vegetables to a serving dish.

11. When the vegetables have come to room temperature, mix in the cherry tomatoes then toss with some fresh olive oil.

Cauliflower With Coconut Sauce (Clean eating, Gluten free, Paleo, Low carb, Dairy free, Vegan)

Preparation time: 15 minutes

Cooking time: 3 minutes

Servings: 4

Ingredients:

1 small head cauliflower, cut into florets

1 bunch asparagus, trimmed, cut into 1 inch pieces

1 carrot, sliced

1 cup coconut milk

1 tablespoon grated fresh ginger

1/2 teaspoon ground cumin

1 tablespoon lemon juice

Salt and pepper to taste

Directions:

1. In a large bowl, combine the coconut milk, ginger, cumin, lemon juice, salt and pepper. Mix well then place in the fridge.

2. Insert the inner pot and the Steamer Tray into your Power Cooker.

3. Add the cauliflower, asparagus, carrot and 1/2 cup of water.

4. Cover the Power Cooker, lock the lid then turn the pressure release valve to closed.

5. Next, press the FISH/VEGETABLE button and adjust the time to 3 minutes.

6. When the time is up, the Power Cooker will switch to KEEP WARM automatically. Turn the pressure release valve to open.

7. Wait until the steam is released completely before opening the cover.

8. Transfer the vegetables to a serving platter. Top with the sauce.

Cabbage Risotto (Gluten Free, Paleo, Vegan)

Preparation time: 10 minutes

Cooking time: 15 minutes

Servings: 4

Ingredients:

1 tablespoon olive oil

2 garlic cloves, minced

1 medium yellow onion, diced

2 cups of arborio rice

3 cups of vegetable broth

1/2 cup white grape juice

1 teaspoon saffron (about 1 large pinch)

1/4 cup fresh thyme or parsley

2 cups finely chopped green cabbage

Salt and pepper, to taste

1 or 2 tablespoons of vegan margarine

1/4 cup lemon juice

Directions:

1. Insert the inner pot into your Power Cooker, press the CHICKEN/MEAT button and add the olive oil. Add onions and garlic. Cook and stir for about 3 minutes.

2. Add the rice and cook with stirring for about 3 minutes.

3. Stir in the vegetable broth, grape juice, saffron, thyme, cabbage, salt and pepper.

4. Cover the Power Cooker, lock the lid then turn the pressure release valve to closed.

5. Next, press the WARM/CANCEL button then choose the FISH/VEGETABLE button and adjust the time to 6 minutes.

6. When the time is up, the Power Cooker will switch to KEEP WARM automatically. Turn the pressure release valve to open.

7. Wait until the steam is released completely before opening the cover.

8. Stir in margarine and lemon juice. Serve warm.

Butternut Squash Risotto (Clean eating, Gluten free)

Enjoy the natural flavor of butternut squash in a creamy and tasty sauce.

Preparation time: 10 minutes

Cooking time: 15 minutes

Servings: 4

Ingredients:

2 tablespoons butter

1/2 onion, minced

2 cups cubed butternut squash

1 teaspoon garlic powder

1 cup Arborio rice

4 cups chicken stock

1/3 cup dry white wine

1/4 cup grated Parmesan cheese

2 tablespoons chopped fresh chives

Salt and ground black pepper to taste

Directions:

1. Insert the inner pot into your Power Cooker, press the CHICKEN/MEAT button and melt the butter. Add onions and cook for 5 minutes.

2. Add the butternut squash, garlic powder and a little salt. Cook for about 5 minutes.

3. Stir in the rice, chicken stock and wine.

4. Cover the Power Cooker, lock the lid then turn the pressure release valve to closed.

5. Next, press the WARM/CANCEL button then choose the FISH/VEGETABLE button and adjust the time to 5 minutes.

6. When the time is up, the Power Cooker will switch to KEEP WARM automatically. Turn the pressure release valve to open.

7. Wait until the steam is released completely before opening the cover.

8. Stir in the grated cheese, season with salt and pepper.

9. Serve, garnished with fresh chives.

Chickpea Soup (Clean eating, Gluten free, Dairy free, Vegan)

Preparation time: 15 minutes

Cooking time: 20 minutes

Servings: 6

Ingredients:

1 1/2 cups dried garbanzo beans (chickpeas), soaked in water overnight, drained

1 tablespoon olive oil

1 large onion, chopped

4 garlic cloves, minced

1 tablespoon snipped rosemary

5 cups vegetable broth

1 (14.5-ounce) can chopped tomatoes

2 bay leaves

1 teaspoon cardamom powder

Salt, to taste

Pepper, to taste

3 tablespoons chopped fresh basil

Directions:

1. Insert the inner pot into your Power Cooker, press the CHICKEN/MEAT button and add the olive oil. Sauté onion in hot oil for about 3 minutes. Add garlic and rosemary then cook for 1 minute.

2. Add the garbanzo beans, vegetable broth, tomatoes, bay leaves, cardamom powder then season to taste with salt and pepper.

3. Cover the Power Cooker, lock the lid then turn the pressure release valve to closed.

4. Next, press the WARM/CANCEL button then press the BEANS/LENTILS button to 15 minutes.

5. When the time is up, the Power Cooker will switch to KEEP WARM automatically. Turn the pressure release valve to open.

6. Wait until the steam is released completely before opening the cover.

7. Remove bay leaves and discard. Use an immersion blender to puree until smooth.

8. Stir in the chopped basil and let simmer on KEEP WARM for about 5 minutes before serving.

Green Beans With Potato And Mushroom (Clean eating, Gluten free, Dairy free, Vegan)

Tender and flavorful green beans with mushrooms, potatoes and tomatoes.

Preparation time: 5 minutes

Cooking time: 15 minutes

Servings: 6

Ingredients:

2 tablespoons olive oil

1 large onion, chopped

3 garlic cloves, minced

2 pounds fresh green beans, trimmed

5 medium potatoes, cubed

4 ounces baby bella or crimini mushrooms, sliced

3 fresh tomatoes, diced

1 cup of water

Salt, to taste

Freshly ground pepper, to taste

Directions:

1. Insert the inner pot into your Power Cooker, press the CHICKEN/MEAT button and add the olive oil. Sauté onions until soft. Add garlic and cook for just 1 minute.

2. Add the rest of the ingredients.

3. Cover the Power Cooker, lock the lid then turn the pressure release valve to closed.

4. Next, press the WARM/CANCEL button then choose the BEANS/LENTILS button and adjust the time to 10 minutes.

5. When the time is up, the Power Cooker will switch to KEEP WARM automatically. Turn the pressure release valve to open.

6. Wait until the steam is released completely before opening the cover.

7. Stir and serve warm.

Mixed Vegetable Soup (Clean eating, Gluten free, Paleo, Low carb, Dairy free, Vegan)

This nutritious soup is cooked within a few minutes.

Preparation time: 10 minutes

Cooking time: 20 minutes

Servings: 6

Ingredients:

1 tablespoon olive oil

1/2 large onion, diced

2 celery ribs, chopped

2 carrots, sliced

1/2 red bell pepper, seeded, sliced

2 cups cabbage, diced

1 (14-5-ounce) can diced tomatoes

1/2 cup tomato puree

5 cups beef or vegetable broth

1 teaspoon ground cumin

1 teaspoon salt

1/2 teaspoon black pepper

8 ounces, frozen green beans

1 large potato, peeled, diced

Directions:

1. Insert the inner pot into your Power Cooker, press the CHICKEN/MEAT button and add the olive oil. Add onion, carrots and celery. Sauté until tender.

2. Add the rest of the ingredients.

3. Cover the Power Cooker, lock the lid then turn the pressure release valve to closed.

4. Next, press the WARM/CANCEL button then press the BEANS/LENTILS button to 15 minutes.

5. When the time is up, the Power Cooker will switch to KEEP WARM automatically. Turn the pressure release valve to open.

6. Wait until the steam is released completely before opening the cover.

7. Serve.

SIDE DISHES

Mashed Acorn Squash (Clean eating, Gluten free, Paleo, Low carb, Vegetarian)

Preparation time: 10 minutes

Cooking time: 24 minutes

Servings: 4-6

Ingredients:

2 acorn squash, stem trimmed, halved, seeded

1/4 teaspoon baking soda

1 teaspoon kosher salt

1/2 cup water

1/2 teaspoon grated nutmeg

2 tablespoons brown sugar

2 tablespoons butter/margarine

Salt, to taste

Pepper, to taste

Directions:

1. Sprinkle baking soda and kosher salt on the cut side of the squash. Insert the Steamer Tray in the Power Cooker, pour in 1/2 cup of water and add the squash.

2. Cover the Power Cooker, lock the lid then turn the pressure release valve to closed.

3. Next, press the BEANS/LENTILS button and adjust the time to 24 minutes.

4. When the time is up, the Power Cooker will switch to KEEP WARM automatically. Turn the pressure release valve to open.

5. Wait until the steam is released completely before opening the cover.

6. Remove the squash and set aside to cool. When the squash is cool, scrape the flesh into a medium bowl.

7. Add the rest of the ingredients and mash with the squash.

Easy Potato Salad (Clean eating, Gluten free, Vegetarian)

Preparation time: 15 minutes

Cooking time: 4 minutes

Servings: 8

Ingredients:

4 large eggs (whole)

6 medium russet potatoes, peeled, cubed

1 1/2 cups water

1 small onion, finely chopped

1 tablespoon mustard

1 cup mayonnaise

1 tablespoon dill pickle juice

2 tablespoons fresh parsley, finely chopped

Salt, to taste

Pepper, to taste

Directions:

1. Insert the Steamer Tray in the Power Cooker. Add the potatoes, water and eggs.

2. Cover the Power Cooker, lock the lid then turn the pressure release valve to closed.

3. Next, press the FISH/VEG./STEAM button to 4 minutes.

4. When the time is up, the Power Cooker will switch to KEEP WARM automatically. Turn the pressure release valve to open.

5. Wait until the steam is released completely before opening the cover.

6. Remove the eggs and place in ice cold water.

7. In a large bowl, mix together onion, mustard, mayonnaise, pickle juice and parsley. Add the potatoes and mix gently.

8. Peel three of the eggs and dice. Stir diced eggs into the potato salad. Season to taste with salt and pepper.

9. Place in the fridge to chill for at least one hour. Slice the remaining egg and place on top.

Steamed Julienned Carrot (Clean eating, Gluten free, Low carb, Dairy free, Vegan)

Preparation time: 5 minutes

Cooking time: 6 minutes

Servings: 4

Ingredients:

1 pound of carrots, peeled, julienned

1 cup water

1/4 cup brown sugar

1/4 cup vegan butter

2 teaspoons lemon juice

1/2 teaspoon cinnamon (optional)

1/4 teaspoon nutmeg (optional)

Directions:

1. Insert the inner pot and the Steamer Tray into your Power Cooker. Add one cup of water and the julienned carrots.

2. Cover the Power Cooker, lock the lid then turn the pressure release valve to closed.

3. Next, press the FISH/VEGETABLE button to 4 minutes.

4. When the time is up, the Power Cooker will switch to KEEP WARM automatically. Turn the pressure release valve to open.

5. Wait until the steam is released completely before opening the cover.

6. Immediately remove the Steamer Tray so that the carrots will stop cooking. Remove carrots and set aside.

7. Drain off most of the cooking water, leaving just enough to cover the bottom of the pan. Stir in the brown sugar and butter.

8. Press the CHICKEN/MEAT button and let simmer until the butter melts. Add the carrots, lemon juice, cinnamon and nutmeg then stir to coat.

9. Press the KEEP WARM button, cover the Power Cooker and let the flavors blend for 5 minutes in the residual heat. Serve.

Brussels Sprouts With Walnuts (Clean eating, Gluten free, Paleo, Low carb, Dairy free, Vegan)
Brighten your dinner table with this colorful side dish.

Preparation time: 5 minutes

Cooking time: 4 minutes

Servings: 6

Ingredients:

1 pound Brussels sprouts

1/2 cup walnuts, toasted, chopped coarsely

2 teaspoons lemon juice

Olive oil

Salt, to taste

Pepper, to taste

Directions:

1. Wash Brussels sprouts, remove outer leaves then trim the stems. Slice the biggest ones in half so they will cook evenly.

2. Insert the inner pot into your Power Cooker, add one cup of water and insert the Steamer Tray. Add the Brussels sprouts to the tray.

3. Cover the Power Cooker, lock the lid then turn the pressure release valve to closed.

4. Next, press the FISH/VEGETABLE button to 4 minutes.

5. When the time is up, the Power Cooker will switch to KEEP WARM automatically. Turn the pressure release valve to open.

6. Wait until the steam is released completely before opening the cover.

7. Transfer the Brussels sprouts to a serving dish. Toss with lemon juice, olive oil, walnuts, salt and pepper.

5. Serve warm.

Orange And Cauliflower Salad (Clean eating, Gluten free, Paleo, Dairy free, Vegan)

A colorful combination of veggies and citrus to brighten up your table.

Preparation time: 5 minutes

Cooking time: 7 minutes

Servings: 4-6

Ingredients:

1 head cauliflower, washed, cut into florets

2 oranges, peeled, seeded, thinly sliced

2 tablespoons parsley, chopped

3 tablespoons golden raisins

1/2 cup sliced green onions

For The Vinaigrette:

Juice from 1 orange

Grated zest from the same orange

1 teaspoon dried tarragon leaves

3 tablespoons extra virgin olive oil

1 tablespoon apple cider vinegar

Salt, to taste

Pepper, to taste

Directions:

1. Make The Vinaigrette: In a small jar, combine orange juice, orange zest, tarragon leaves, olive oil, vinegar, salt and pepper. Close the jar, shake well and set aside.

2. Insert the inner pot into your Power Cooker, add one cup of water and insert the Steamer Tray. Add the cauliflower florets to the tray.

3. Cover the Power Cooker, lock the lid then turn the pressure release valve to closed.

4. Next, press the FISH/VEGETABLE button and adjust the time to 7 minutes.

5. When the time is up, the Power Cooker will switch to KEEP WARM automatically. Turn the pressure release valve to open.

6. Wait until the steam is released completely before opening the cover.

7. Arrange the cauliflower florets on a serving dish then add the sliced orange, parsley, raisins and green onions. Shake the vinaigrette again and pour it on top.

Super Easy Refried Beans (Clean eating, Gluten free, Dairy free, Vegan)

Preparation time: 15 minutes

Cooking time: 45 minutes

Servings: 6

Ingredients:

2 cups dried pinto beans, sorted, rinsed (You don't have to soak)

2 tablespoons vegetable oil

1 medium onion, chopped roughly

4 garlic cloves, chopped roughly

1/2 cup chopped cilantro

1 teaspoon cumin

1/2 teaspoon chipotle powder

1 teaspoon paprika

3 1/2 cups water

Salt, to taste

Directions:

1. Insert the inner pot into your Power Cooker, press the CHICKEN/MEAT button and add the vegetable oil. Add the onion, garlic and cilantro. Cook and stir until onions are tender.

2. Stir in the beans and remaining ingredients.

3. Cover the Power Cooker, lock the lid then turn the pressure release valve to closed.

4. Next, press the WARM/CANCEL button then choose the SOUP/STEW button and adjust the time to 35 minutes.

5. When the time is up, the Power Cooker will switch to KEEP WARM automatically. Turn the pressure release valve to open.

6. Wait until the steam is released completely before opening the cover.

7. Taste the beans and adjust seasoning as necessary. If you want it very thick, drain some of the cooking liquid.

8. Mash with a potato masher or immersion blender until smooth.

Broccoli, Raisins And Cherries (Clean eating, Gluten free, Paleo, Low carb, Dairy free, Vegan)

This is a great accompaniment to any main dish.

Preparation time: 5 minutes

Cooking time: 2 minutes

Servings: 4

Ingredients:

1 head broccoli, cut into florets

1 tablespoon lemon juice

1 cup water

1/4 cup raisins

1/4 cup dried cherries

2 garlic cloves, minced

1 medium onion, chopped finely

1 teaspoon olive oil

2 tablespoons red wine vinegar

1/8 teaspoon cayenne pepper

Directions:

1. Insert the inner pot into your Power Cooker. Pour in water and lemon juice then add the broccoli.

2. Cover the Power Cooker, lock the lid then turn the pressure release valve to closed.

3. Next, press the FISH/VEGETABLE button to 2 minutes.

4. When the time is up, the Power Cooker will switch to KEEP WARM automatically. Turn the pressure release valve to open.

5. Wait until the steam is released completely before opening the cover.

6. In a large bowl, combine raisins, cherries, garlic, onion, olive oil, vinegar and cayenne pepper. Mix together very well.

4. Add the broccoli and toss.

Quinoa Salad (Clean eating, Gluten free, Dairy free, Vegan)

Preparation time: 10 minutes

Cooking time: 1 minute

Servings: 6

Ingredients:

1 cup quinoa, rinsed

1 1/2 cups water

1 garlic clove, minced

1/2 teaspoon salt

1 cucumber, seeded, diced finely

1 large roma tomato, diced finely

1 bell pepper, diced finely

1/2 cup thinly sliced scallions

1 bunch parsley, minced

1 ripe avocado, peeled, pitted, diced

3 tablespoons freshly squeezed lime juice

2 tablespoons vegetable broth

Directions:

1. Insert the inner pot into your Power Cooker then add the quinoa, water, garlic and salt.

2. Cover the Power Cooker, lock the lid then turn the pressure release valve to closed.

3. Next, press the FISH/VEGETABLE button to 4 minutes.

4. When the time is up, the Power Cooker will switch to KEEP WARM automatically. Turn the pressure release valve to open.

5. Wait until the steam is released completely before opening the cover.

6. Fluff the quinoa and let cool.

7. Combine the rest of the ingredients in a large bowl and mix well. Add the quinoa and mix again.

Carrots And Chicory Salad (Clean eating, Gluten free, Paleo, Low carb, Dairy free, Vegan)

Preparation time: 10 minutes

Cooking time: 10 minutes

Servings: 4

Ingredients:

1 bunch of chicory

1 large carrot, peeled, grated

1 garlic clove, minced

1 sprig thyme

1 cup vegetable broth

Salt, to taste

Pepper, to taste

3 tablespoons olive oil

2 tablespoons lemon juice

1 tablespoon balsamic vinegar

Directions:

1. Rinse the chicory in 2-3 changes of water. Spin dry and tear into pieces.

2. Insert the inner pot into your Power Cooker, press the CHICKEN/MEAT button and add the olive oil. Add the carrots and cook for 2-3 minutes.

3. Add the garlic and thyme; cook for 1 minute then stir in the chicory. Add the vegetable broth then season with salt and pepper.

4. Cover the Power Cooker, lock the lid then turn the pressure release valve to closed.

5. Next, press the WARM/CANCEL button then choose the BEANS/LENTILS button (5 minutes).

6. When the time is up, the Power Cooker will switch to KEEP WARM automatically. Turn the pressure release valve to open.

7. Wait until the steam is released completely before opening the cover.

8.Open the lid, remove and discard the thyme.

9. Using a slotted spoon, transfer chicory and carrots to a bowl. Add the remaining olive oil, balsamic vinegar and lemon juice. Toss to thoroughly combine.

DESSERTS

Applesauce (Clean eating, Gluten free, Dairy free, Vegan)

Preparation time: 10 minutes

Cooking time: 4 minutes

Servings: Yields 4 cups

Ingredients:

3 pounds apples, peeled, cored, sliced

1/4 cup sugar

1/2 cups apple juice or apple cider

Pinch of salt

1/2 teaspoon ground cardamom

1/2 teaspoon ground cinnamon

1 tablespoon lemon juice

Directions:

1. Insert the inner pot into your Power Cooker and add all the ingredients.

2. Cover the Power Cooker, lock the lid then turn the pressure release valve to closed.

3. Next, press the FISH/VEGETABLE to 4 minutes.

4. When the time is up, the Power Cooker will switch to KEEP WARM automatically. Turn the pressure release valve to open.

5. Wait until the steam is released completely before opening the cover.

6. Use an immersion blender or regular blender to blend to desired consistency.

Rice Pudding (Clean eating, Gluten free)

The Power Cooker provides a quicker way to cook rice pudding.

Preparation time: 10 minutes

Cooking time: 13 minutes

Servings: 6-8

Ingredients:

1 tablespoon butter

1 cup long-grain rice, uncooked

1 1/2 cups water

2 cups whole milk, divided

1/2 teaspoon salt

1/2 cup sugar

1 egg

1/4 cup cream

1 teaspoon vanilla extract

Cinnamon, to taste

Directions:

1. Insert the inner pot into your Power Cooker, press the CHICKEN/MEAT button and add the butter.

2. When the butter melts, stir in the rice, milk, water, salt and sugar.

3. Cover the Power Cooker, lock the lid then turn the pressure release valve to closed.

4. Next, press the WARM/CANCEL button then choose the RICE/RISOTTO button and adjust the time to 8 minutes.

5. When the time is up, the Power Cooker will switch to KEEP WARM automatically. Turn the pressure release valve to open.

6. Wait until the steam is released completely before opening the cover.

7. Beat the egg in a small bowl then whisk in cream and vanilla. Stir the mixture into the Power Cooker.

8. Select the CHICKEN/MEAT button and cook, uncovered until the rice starts to bubble then turn off the Power Cooker.

9. Let the pudding stand for about 10 minutes with occasional stirring.

10. Serve, sprinkled with cinnamon.

Pear In Honey Cranberry Sauce (Clean eating, Gluten free, Vegetarian)

Preparation time: 10 minutes

Cooking time: 10 minutes

Servings: 10

Ingredients:

3 pears, peeled, cored, diced

1 (12-ounce) package cranberries (fresh or frozen)

3/4 cup hot water

1 cup honey

1/2 cup white sugar

1 clove

1/2 teaspoon ground nutmeg

1 pinch of cinnamon

Directions:

1. Insert the inner pot into your Power Cooker then add hot water, honey, sugar and clove. Stir until the sugar dissolves.

2. Stir in the nutmeg and cinnamon then add the pears and cranberries.

3. Cover the Power Cooker, lock the lid then turn the pressure release valve to closed.

4. Next, press the WARM/CANCEL button then choose the BEANS/LENTILS button and adjust the time to 6 minutes.

5. When the time is up, the Power Cooker will switch to KEEP WARM automatically. Turn the pressure release valve to open.

6. Wait until the steam is released completely before opening the cover.

Dried Fruits In Red Wine Sauce (Clean eating, Gluten free, Dairy free, Vegan)

Preparation time: 10 minutes

Cooking time: 10 minutes

Servings: 6

Ingredients:

1 medium onion, diced

1 garlic clove, minced

2 tablespoon olive oil

1 cup dried apricots

1 cup dried peaches

1 cup dried figs

1 1/2 cup red wine

1/2 cup water

3/4 cup packed brown sugar

2 lemon slices

1 cinnamon stick

Salt and pepper, to taste (optional)

Directions:

1. Cut the dried fruits into smaller pieces.

2. Insert the inner pot into your Power Cooker, press the CHICKEN/MEAT button and add the olive oil. Sauté onion and garlic for about 5 minutes.

3. Add the rest of the ingredients. Bring to a boil and stir until the sugar dissolves.

4. Cover the Power Cooker, lock the lid then turn the pressure release valve to closed.

5. Next, press the WARM/CANCEL button then choose the BEANS/LENTILS button (5 minutes).

6. When the time is up, the Power Cooker will switch to KEEP WARM automatically. Turn the pressure release valve to open.

7. Wait until the steam is released completely before opening the cover.

8. Serve warm.

Candied Lemon Peels (Clean eating, Gluten free, Dairy free, Vegan)

This delicious dessert can be made with any citrus fruit - lemon, orange, grapefruit and so on.

Preparation time: 20 minutes

Cooking time: 20 minutes

Servings: 30

Ingredients:

6 (thick-skinned) organic lemons

3 cups sugar, divided

6 cups water, divided

Directions:

1. Cut top and bottom off each lemon then use a vegetable peeler to peel the skin. You can juice the lemon and reserve the juice for other recipes.

2. Insert the inner pot into your Power Cooker. Add the lemon peels and 4 cups of water.

3. Cover the Power Cooker, lock the lid then turn the pressure release valve to closed.

4. Next, press the WARM/CANCEL button then choose the FISH/VEGETABLE button and adjust the time to 3 minutes.

5. When the time is up, the Power Cooker will switch to KEEP WARM automatically. Turn the pressure release valve to open.

6. Wait until the steam is released completely before opening the cover.

7. Drain the water then rinse the lemon peels with fresh cold water. Rinse the inner Pot as well.

8. Add 2 1/2 cups of sugar to the lemon peels then add 1 1/2 or 2 cups of water. Choose the CHICKEN/MEAT button and cook uncovered with occasional stirring, for about 5 minutes or until sugar melts.

9. Again, cover the Power Cooker, lock the lid then turn the pressure release valve to closed.

10. Next, press the WARM/CANCEL button then press the FISH/VEGETABLE button to 10 minutes.

11. When the time is up, the Power Cooker will switch to KEEP WARM automatically. Turn the pressure release valve to open. Wait until the steam is released completely before opening the cover.

12. Use a slotted spoon to transfer the peels to parchment paper and let cool for about 20 minutes.

13. Spread the remaining sugar on a wide plate. Working in batches, toss lemon peels with sugar and shake off excess. Transfer to a sheet pan and place in the fridge to dry for at least 5 hours.

14. Transfer to glass jars and store in the refrigerator for 2-3 months.

Power Cooker Baked Apples (Clean eating, Gluten free, Dairy free, Vegan)

Preparation time: 5 minutes

Cooking time: 10 minutes

Servings: 4-5

Ingredients:

4-5 apples

1 1/2 cup of water

1/2 cup sugar or other sweetener

1/2 cup of dates, chopped roughly

1/4 cup walnuts or raisins, chopped roughly

2 tablespoons goji berries

1 teaspoon cinnamon powder

1 pinch of ginger (optional)

Directions:

1. Core the apples and cut off the top and bottom.

2. Insert the inner pot into your Power Cooker then add the apples.

3. Pour in the water then add sugar, dates, nuts, goji berries, cinnamon and ginger.

4. Cover the Power Cooker, lock the lid then turn the pressure release valve to closed.

5. Next, press the FISH/VEGETABLE button to 10 minutes.

6. When the time is up, the Power Cooker will switch to KEEP WARM automatically. Turn the pressure release valve to open.

7. Wait until the steam is released completely before opening the cover.

8. Serve apples with the cooking liquid.

Tapioca Pudding (Clean eating, Gluten free, Dairy free, Vegan)

It is not necessary to presoak the tapioca pearls.

Preparation time: 5 minutes

Cooking time: 15 minutes

Servings: 4

Ingredients:

1/3 cup small tapioca pearls

1 1/4 cups water

1 1/4 cups unsweetened almond milk

4 tablespoons sweetener of choice (granulated sugar, unrefined cane sugar, agave etc)

1/2 teaspoon vanilla extract

1 teaspoon corn starch

Directions:

1. Rinse the tapioca pearls and drain.

2. Insert the inner pot into your Power Cooker, then add the tapioca pearls and water.

3. Cover the Power Cooker, lock the lid then turn the pressure release valve to closed.

4. Next, press the RICE/RISOTTO button and adjust the time to 8 minutes.

5. When the time is up, the Power Cooker will switch to KEEP WARM automatically. Turn the pressure release valve to open.

6. Wait until the steam is released completely before opening the cover.

7. Stir in the almond milk, sweetener and the corn starch.

5. Press the CHICKEN/MEAT button and let simmer uncovered, stirring frequently until the mixture just starts boiling. Stir in the vanilla extract and turn off the Power Cooker.

6. Let cool to room temperature with occasional stirring as it thickens.

7. Pour into serving dishes, cover and chill in the fridge for about 2 hours before serving.

Spicy Apple Crunch (Clean eating)
You can also make this with peaches instead of apples.

Preparation time: 10 minutes

Cooking time: 17 minutes

Servings: 3

Ingredients:

1 cup dry bread crumbs (whole grain bread)

1/2 teaspoon cinnamon

1/4 cup sugar

1 lemon (juice and zest)

3 apples, sliced

1/4 cup butter, melted

1 1/2 cups water

Directions:

1. Coat a 6-inch baking dish with butter.

2. In a bowl, combine bread crumbs, cinnamon, sugar, lemon juice and lemon zest.

3. Place a single layer of apple slices in the baking dish, spread with bread crumbs mixture. Continue layering apple slices and bread crumbs mixture until you run out.

4. Pour melted butter over everything then firmly cover the baking dish with foil.

5. Insert the inner pot into your Power Cooker and add 1 1/2 cups of water. Place the baking dish inside.

6. Cover the Power Cooker, lock the lid then turn the pressure release valve to closed.

7. Next, press the BEANS/LENTILS button and adjust the time to 17 minutes.

8. When the time is up, the Power Cooker will switch to KEEP WARM automatically. Turn the pressure release valve to open.

9. Wait until the steam is released completely before opening the cover.

10. Take out the baking dish and remove the foil. Transfer to the fridge to cool.

END

Made in the USA
Lexington, KY
12 June 2017